ROONEY TUNES

ROONEY TUNES

MIKE PARRY

WARRINGTON BOROUGH COUNCIL	
Bertrams	05.08.06
796.334 RS	£17.99

JOHN BLAKE

Published by John Blake Publishing Ltd,
3 Bramber Court, 2 Bramber Road,
London W14 9PB, England

www.blake.co.uk

First published in hardback in 2006

ISBN 1 84454 268 8

British Library Cataloguing-in-Publication Data:

A catalogue record for this book is available from the British Library.

Design by www.envydesign.co.uk

Printed in Great Britain by Creative Print & Design, Wales

1 3 5 7 9 10 8 6 4 2

Papers used by John Blake Publishing are natural, recyclable products made
from wood grown in sustainable forests. The manufacturing processes
conform to the environmental regulations of the country of origin.

Photographs courtesy of Getty Images, Rex Features, Clevamedia, Empics
and John Ingledew

Every attempt has been made to contact the relevant copyright-holders,
but some were unobtainable. We would be grateful if the appropriate
people could contact us.

This book is dedicated to the memory of
William Ralph Dean and
Rear Admiral Sir Horatio Nelson.

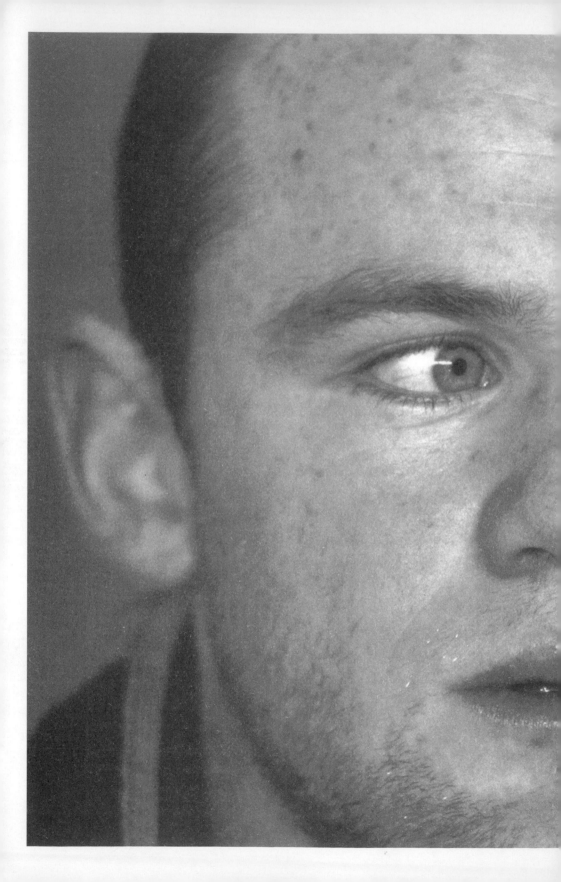

CONTENTS

PROLOGUE

IT WAS THE most innocuous challenge of the season. Wayne Rooney was sprinting for a ball with Chelsea defender Paulo Ferreira when he went down and rolled across the grass.

Even before he came to a halt the Manchester United protégé was waving his arm, indicating alarm.

As he stopped, he propped himself up and let out an anguished scream. His face was contorted into a mask that reminded those watching of the famous painting by Munch, *The Scream*.

His mouth was as wide open as it could be, a circular cavern in his face emitting more than pain. It was an expression of terror and despair and dawning frustration. It was the split second realisation that the electric shock-like stab that he had just felt in his right foot must indicate a broken bone.

The incident had happened after exactly seventy eight minutes and thirty five seconds of the third-to-last game of the season and it would change the course of world football.

Judging by Rooney's expression he knew right away that he had sustained an injury that was similar to the broken metatarsal that had ended his Euro 2004 campaign two years earlier.

In futility, he grabbed at his right ankle. Then his hand moved down to the toe of his boot. He seemed to be massaging the head of the blue boot as though he could rub his injury better.

A few days earlier he had posed with his new footwear in a promotion with the sports company Nike. He was launching a new brand – Total 90 Supremacy – which he was planning to wear at the World Cup. Nike, quick to clarify their own interests, stated: 'There is no indication there is a problem with the boot.' Like we cared about the boot.

On the pitch at Chelsea's Stamford Bridge on the day that the Blues clinched the Premiership, Rooney was calmed down by team-mates and coaches who ran out to him and made him lie motionless on the turf.

You could see the continuing distress in his face. At one point his eyes welled up, either with shock, pain or distress. He continually rubbed his stubbled face with his hands as he was trying to think through the consequences of what had just happened.

England's first game at Germany 06 against Paraguay was due to kick-off exactly six weeks later. Six weeks.

The training staff were examining his foot. With concern clearly visible on their faces, they waved for a stretcher. Four men ran onto the field with the orange cradle-like contraption.

His boot had been gently removed from his right foot. Now he was on the stretcher. He was strapped on – and as he was carried from the pitch there was a muted silence in the stadium. Speculation began and immediately reached fever-point. Many of us hoped it might just be a twisted ankle. Many prayers were muttered under our breaths.

Amongst the spectators was England coach Sven-Goran Eriksson. Some of his England internationals were playing for Chelsea; John Terry and Frank Lampard stood huddled together on the pitch fifty yards away clearly deep in thought about the ramifications on England's World Cup challenge.

It should have been a day of ecstatic celebration for Chelsea fans. Five minutes before the Rooney injury their team had scored a third goal to seal victory and give them their second consecutive Premiership title. But even to these fans, for a decade arch-rivals of Manchester United, there was a realisation that England's World Cup ambitions were under threat.

As the final whistle blew, the home fans forgot about Rooney for the moment and returned to the business of celebrating their magnificent achievement.

John Terry, who had injured his foot when Rooney tackled him earlier in the game, limped off down the tunnel to find out what he could about his international team-mate.

He approached the United dressing-room but found it closed. There were a number of security guards on the door.

It was reported that at one stage the Chelsea manager Jose Mourinho had had a quick word with a United official who had said that the injury wouldn't affect Rooney's World Cup.

If only. In those early minutes after such a huge incident takes place there is always information and counter-information flying about. But nobody really knew.

As the celebrations were going on above, doctors and physios were urgently examining the most prized right foot in English football.

A break was suspected.

An hour later Rooney, using crutches and with his right foot covered, struggled on to the team bus. He was wearing his black Manchester United blazer with the club crest on the pocket. Abject despair was written all over his face.

When he got back to Old Trafford he was given an initial scan. At 9.30pm that evening the news was then released that he had broken the fourth metatarsal and that he would be out for six weeks. In Portugal two years earlier he had broken the fifth bone.

Even though it had been widely expected, it was a catastrophic confirmation of everybody's worst fears. Manchester United had released the information after informing the England coach.

What did six weeks mean? Six weeks until he was fit to play again? Six weeks until he could train again?

Eyes darted to the calendar. Could he be fit for the third qualifying game against Sweden – or maybe the first knock-out game on June 25?

Hours after the announcement Eriksson issued a statement making it clear that he would be taking

Rooney to Germany while there was still some chance he could play in the later games.

He said: 'Wayne is a world-class player and we will give him every opportunity to play in the finals.'

The rules for squad membership mean that managers can be given breathing space when considering injuries. An initial list was submitted to FIFA on May 8, which included the name all were looking out for – Wayne Rooney. That list then had to be whittled down to 23 players by May 15 with the World Cup starting on June 9. Any player carrying an injury can be replaced up to 24 hours before his country's first game in the competition.

Sven's immediate decision to assure Rooney that he would be part of the squad was soon being questioned by Sir Alex Ferguson.

The Manchester United boss called for a reality check. He said: 'We have to be sure we don't build up people's expectations too much. That is what is happening at the moment. Sven-Goran Eriksson, saying that he will take Wayne to Germany, fit or not, was something we didn't want to hear. This club will do absolutely everything to get the boy there. But if he is not fit, he is not going.

'The idea that he will be right in six weeks and then have another two weeks to get fit for the quarter-finals is a wild dream. Wayne has to make a proper recovery from this injury.

'All the other players there will have been playing for the previous two months. And they will all be honed to one hundred per cent fitness. It's folly to say a boy should come back after six weeks and then play in the World Cup.'

Some believed that by speaking out Sir Alex was

making it clear that Manchester United's interests were a priority in the issue. Others believed he was simply being pragmatic and reminding the country that these sort of injuries do not repair themselves quickly. Following the break in Lisbon which ended his participation in Portugal 04, Wayne did not play again for fourteen weeks.

None of the eight other England players who have had a broken metatarsal were fit to play again inside eight weeks. England striker Michael Owen needed nearly eighteen weeks before he played a part in another game.

Within three days of the disaster Rooney spoke to the world. He momentarily and bravely put his devastation behind him to give fans the message that though his foot was broken, his spirit was not.

Sitting with his right leg, cast on his foot, resting on a chair, he indicated he had not given up on his World Cup dream, saying: 'You've just got to get on with it and be positive. I'll be trying to get myself fit as soon as possible.

'I'm obviously devastated but I'll be giving myself the best possible chance. It's really horrible but I'm in great hands at United and the physio team that I have got here will give me the best possible chance.'

Sadly, twenty four hours later, it was revealed that he had suffered more than one fracture to his bone.

Sven-Goran Eriksson's reaction to that news summed up the fears of the whole country: 'Miracles happen now and then, but I don't really know.' None of us did.

Wayne Rooney remained philosophical about the injury that appeared to have shattered his World Cup dreams. He realised that the verdict on his fitness would have to come on a day-by-day, game-by-game basis as

Wayne Rooney was named as the PFA Young Player of the Year for the second consecutive time at the 2006 awards. He picked up the trophy at the Grosvenor House Hotel from 1966 World Cup winner Alan Ball. In accepting his award, Rooney said: 'It's a great honour to get it twice. It's also wonderful to receive it from a man like Alan Ball who has won the biggest prize. It is a tremendous honour.' Rooney was smiling broadly and looked very composed in his acceptance speech. He had also been short-listed for the senior PFA Player of the Year Award which went to his England team-mate, Liverpool's Steven Gerrard.

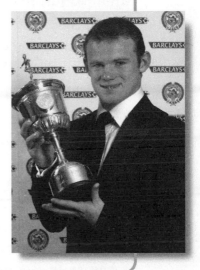

the tournament progressed, with little chance of him taking part in the group stage.

However, one uplifting moment came for him just days after breaking his foot when he was named Manchester United's Fans' Player of the Year, adding to the PFA Young Player of the Year award which he received only days before, on April 23.

He hobbled to the ceremony on crutches with his right foot encased in the soft cast which looks more like a giant white boot. Accepting the award, he said: 'If it is not to be for me this time then I'm sure there will be a lot more tournaments.

'I hope to get fit for this one because as a young lad, it is every player's ambition to play in a World Cup. I have to be strong and I'm still hoping. But if not then it's not the end of the world.

'Football is a physical game and injuries happen. Mine has just happened at a bad time. I am a strong lad though, and I have had great support and I hope I can come back and get fit.'

England boss Sven-Goran Eriksson held on to his unshakeable belief in his boy wonder. He said he would take Rooney as a valuable member of the 23-man squad even if the star striker was going to be fit for only one game – the final.

And the England team doctor never wavered from his prognosis that Rooney's injury gave him a chance to play in the finals. Leif Sward said: 'I kept my hopes high by being an optimist by nature.'

And with Rooney's brave face looking increasingly positive, and with his foot in the best of medical hands, there was still a chance...

PREFACE BY ANDY TOWNSEND

THERE IS NOTHING quiet about Porky Parry when he's talking about something in which he believes as strongly as he believes in the raw talent of Wayne Rooney.

He's not prepared to allow others any doubt and that is why his cry of 'Roooooooney!' will reach a crescendo whatever happens.

What Mike loves about Rooney is the way he goes about his business, his passion for the game, his hunger and desire to be a winner and his outstanding natural ability to get everyone on the edge of their seat.

It doesn't matter whether you're watching from your living room or the stands – the effect is the same.

Like all special players before him, he has his flaws, particularly his competitive nature that sometimes seems in danger of boiling over, but it's this unpredictability that makes him box office and not since Gazza in the 90s have we seen someone who can dominate games for England on the world stage with such raw talent.

Rooney will be at the centre of world speculation and media attention, whether he's wearing a football shirt or a Prada suit and a leg cast. Everybody will want a bit of him off the field and every defender will want to kick him up in the air on the field.

The tantalising question with the boy is to find out just what he can achieve. He started in spectacular fashion at Euro 2004 and even in two years he has made gigantic strides in his development. How about that at just 20 years of age?

Ever since my broadcasting pal Mike first clapped eyes on this young man wearing the blue of his beloved Everton, he has followed his every run, pass, tackle, goal and of course the odd yellow and red.

I have tried to pin Mike down on why he feels so supportive of Rooney and it is because he genuinely believes Rooney could be the best footballer ever.

If that comes to pass remember who told you first!

I love this book for its refusal to consider any flaw in the Rooney portfolio. The author's belief in the brilliance of one man is unquestionable.

Andy Townsend is a former professional footballer with Aston Villa, Chelsea, Middlesbrough and West Bromwich Albion, and was skipper of the Republic of Ireland team at two World Cups. He is now an expert commentator and analyst on ITV1.

FOREWORD BY ALAN BRAZIL

I DISTINCTLY REMEMBER the moment I first heard the name 'Wayne Rooney'.

Mike Parry and I had just arrived at Aintree Racecourse on the day of the 2001 Grand National. That morning, we had been broadcasting our breakfast show on talkSPORT from a pub in Liverpool city centre in the build-up to the big race.

A car took us out to the track, where we were greeted by Charlie MacCann, our racing correspondent, who is now head of PR for Littlewoods Bet Direct.

Charlie, a tall, avuncular man is, in addition to being a renowned expert in betting and bloodstock matters, a lifelong Everton fan.

A native of Merseyside, he lives within binocular distance of the main stand at Aintree and it could be said that, with his social and business connections, he is regarded as something of an 'insider' when it comes to his beloved football club.

Mike, who had been brought up just down the road in Chester, is an exiled Everton fan now living in Surrey, so whenever the two of them get together, the talk is all about Everton.

'Porky' – the term I saddled Mike with when we first started working together in radio in the late 90s – has an insatiable appetite for news about their club.

Normally when I see the two of them getting together, I grab myself a bottle of champagne and hover in the background for an hour or two while they swap notes. On this particular day, I heard Mike fire the question: 'How is the boy doing?'

Charlie replied, 'From what I'm hearing, it's just sensational. It's even better than we thought. Talk about one for the future. He could very soon be one for the present.'

As a schoolboy footballer myself who had a record-breaking season with Celtic Boys Club, I was intrigued. 'Who's this?' I asked.

'Wayne Rooney,' they replied in unison.

Charlie went on to explain that he was the most talked-about young footballer on Merseyside since Michael Owen and that many rated him as even better than the then-Liverpool idol.

I'd more or less forgotten that conversation until about eighteen months later. Porky and I had finished our Saturday morning breakfast show and were being entertained for lunch in a London casino.

It was quite a long lunch and the Sky TV Saturday afternoon programme, hosted by our pal Jeff Stelling, was on a screen in the restaurant.

There was a particular interest in the Everton vs

Arsenal fixture because most of the people we were with were 'Gooners' and their club were the current Premiership champions.

In addition, Arsenal were on a long run of unbeaten games and were seeking to extend that sequence even further. Nobody anticipated any problems that afternoon, because Everton had seen better days and had been struggling to re-establish themselves as a top club for the past few years.

News came through of another goal at Goodison Park. Everybody assumed that Arsenal had grabbed a very late winner and the reporter at Everton's ground suddenly came on the screen. He was very excited, but we couldn't actually hear anything. Then the scoreline came up: Everton 2 Arsenal 1.

Porky, of course, went mad. He was jumping up and down and berating our hosts with the 'southern softies' tag.

The other fans around us asked each other if they were reading it right. Arsenal, who had been unbeaten for nearly a calendar year, were suddenly losing to what was then perceived as not a very good team. There were a lot of puzzled-looking people. Then the name of the scorer came up. Rooney.

Mike went into overdrive and let out a scream similar to the sort of thing that Tarzan would have emitted in the jungle when he found Jane.

'Wayne Rooney! ... Wonder kid! ... Greatest young talent in the world,' he said, over and over again.

One of the diners uttered the immortal phrase, 'Who's Wayne Rooney?'

Mike gave him a full explanation.

'Beaten by some Scouser kid,' said another.

By now everybody wanted to know more. We crowded around the telly, demanded that the sound be turned up and listened to Arsenal manager Arsène Wenger being interviewed immediately after the game.

Instead of ruing his own team's luck, he was talking in glowing terms about Everton's scorer. We were picking up snatches of the conversation: 'Greatest young talent ... never seen anything like it in England ...'

And so, amongst our group, the Rooney legend was born.

The word 'fanatic' is often used too lightly, but Mike became a fanatical fan. He beat the Rooney drum to the point where people would have happily beaten him to death.

It only took until the following February that the Everton protégé was playing for England. He made his debut against Australia at Upton Park.

And for months afterwards, Mike would drag our breakfast show all over the country to wherever England were playing that night so that he wouldn't miss a Rooney appearance. The following day, we would broadcast from a temporary studio in a hotel suite.

I remember in particular the England game against Turkey at Sunderland, just a couple of months after Rooney's debut.

During my career I played for Scotland, so my idea of fun is not to sit in a stadium full of Englishmen urging the team on to qualify for the European Championships. But I wanted to watch the game on the telly just to be able to form an opinion of the player's ability for myself: after about ten minutes I knew I was watching a phenomenon.

The sheer audacity of his play for such a young boy against hardened Turkish internationals – never known to show restraint when a set of six studs will do – was sensational.

Rooney was quite rightly named Man of the Match and, when Porky got back to the hotel, I was able to put the fever that had gripped him about Wayne Rooney into perspective for the first time.

A lady listener to our show sent Mike a ceramic lapel badge with an image of the young footballer's face. Around the edge it said: 'Wayne Rooney – England's Youngest Player. Youth is Temporary. Class is Forever.'

It is forged in blue and white and my broadcasting pal would wear it whenever we were at a function. When we were doing after-dinner speeches or meeting potential sponsors for our show he always wore it.

I called it 'that bloody badge' and I used to apologise mockingly to people on his behalf. But he never found it funny. He used to say in all seriousness that any Englishmen should be as proud of Wayne Rooney as he is.

The day after Rooney's transfer was completed to Manchester United, he arrived at work minus the badge. However, I'm told he still wears it when he is watching England.

When I once asked him about the move, he said, 'We spawned him. We developed him and gave him to England and the world. He was brought up in blue. It doesn't matter what happens in the future. Nobody can change that.'

And I know from personal experience that nobody is ever going to change Mike Parry's view that Rooney is the greatest footballer in the world.

ROONEY TUNES

Alan Brazil was formerly a professional footballer with Ipswich Town, Tottenham Hotspur, Manchester United and Scotland and is now an award-winning breakfast show host of talkSPORT Radio.

ONE

WAYNE ROONEY
SAVED MY LIFE

THREE DOCTORS SAT in armchairs around my bed.

These guys were the best in the world. One was a consultant cardiologist and the other two were the surgeons who were going to carry out the heart transplant that was necessary to save my life.

I had already been told by other specialists that my heart would probably not last more than three months, and with that possibility in mind, the discussion turned to whether or not I was going to need an artificial heart. There are not enough donor hearts to go around for those who need them and a patient may have to wait up to a year for a transplant.

I wasn't going to last anything like as long as that, so there was the possibility that I was going to have to have a Left Ventricular Assist Device. It was not a prospect I relished one bit.

I had acute heart failure and the left side of my heart had more or less packed in. It meant that I was struggling along with about one-third of my ticker working, mainly on the right-hand side of the organ. The side-effects of this were constant nausea, breathlessness and almost total immobility.

It was a pretty dismal existence, but even though I felt so dreadfully ill, I still wasn't looking forward to being given the LVAD.

An LVAD is a mechanical device that is inserted into your heart. It simulates the work that the heart should be doing. In my condition – which had been diagnosed as dilated cardiomyopathy – a large part of your heart has become like a flabby old balloon; it has stretched out, but won't come in again as a reflex.

The problem with the LVAD is that you are permanently attached to a battery and a pump – which is the size of a small suitcase and which you have to push around in front of you on a trolley – by a tube that runs from your chest: when you move, your pump goes with you. If you go to the loo, it goes with you; and when you sleep, it clanks away by your side all night.

One poor chap in my unit had two of these devices, one for each side of his heart. Was this to be my fate?

I listened as the doctors debated the issue. I was propped up in a bed in my own room at Harefield Hospital in Middlesex, the world's top cardio-thoracic centre, wired up to a heart-monitoring machine that made it impossible to go anywhere.

It was a glorious July day outside and the sunshine lit up the beautifully tended grounds of Harefield. The wind rustled the rhododendron bushes as rabbits played on the grass. I wondered when I would next be able to go outside … if ever.

I had no self-pity. I had completely come to terms with my situation. It could have happened to anybody, but it happened to me. I had already had a great life and there were plenty of people around who were even worse off than me. Nevertheless, things were looking very grim and my immediate future was nothing but bleak.

As I lay there looking out of the window, I saw my sister, Adrienne, arrive in her car. The doctors concluded their consultation and shuffled off.

The hospital was brilliant about visitors and they could come at any time. Since I became ill, my family had been terribly supportive and it didn't surprise me to see her.

She opened the back door of her car and was struggling to get something out. I couldn't make out what she was doing, but suddenly a huge frame, the size of a window, appeared in her hands. She staggered towards the entrance and, within a few minutes, she was standing at the entrance to my room with what I thought was a painting.

Smiling broadly, she said hello and added, 'You'll never guess what I have got for you here.'

I didn't have a lot of enthusiasm for presents. My room was already full of junk, like mobile DVD players, and books, so trying to muster a smile, I said airily, 'What's that then?'

'You're not going to believe this,' she said, and turned the frame around.

It was a plain white t-shirt and what immediately caught the eye was a very distinctive logo in orange and black that read 'HOW LO'.

HOW LO are an organisation that hold reverse auctions, where you have to get the lowest unique bid rather than the highest, and my radio station, talkSPORT, had been doing business with them for some time.

While very grateful to them for their thoughts, I was trying to figure out why I had been sent a framed t-shirt. Adrienne moved towards my bed, pointed at the middle of the shirt and said: 'Look.' Somebody had scribbled on it in felt-tipped pen.

I looked closely and a wave of realisation started to sweep over me. A smile soon spread across my face and

The author proudly showing off his prized possession – the get-well t-shirt signed by Wayne.

I became elated. The words said: 'To Mike, Best Wishes, Get Well Soon – Wayne Rooney.'

I couldn't believe it. The man who I had already branded the greatest footballer in the world had sent me a personal get-well-soon card on one of his t-shirts.

Two of our sales girls had been doing a promotion with HOW LO at the same time as Rooney. When he heard who they worked for, he asked them whether it was the same talkSPORT that I worked for. He had apparently read in the newspapers that I had been struck down with my heart and also knew that I was a huge supporter of his.

When the girls said yes, he picked up the shirt, scribbled his message on it and said, 'Give that to Mike. I hope he's okay.'

They were gob-smacked and so was I. The shirt had been sent to my home and my sister had got it framed. She knew it would give me a terrific lift and she was absolutely right.

I started shouting for the nurses. I wanted to tell somebody that Wayne Rooney had just sent me the most amazing get-well-soon card.

Ever since I had been in hospital, I had been getting bag-loads of cards from well-wishers from all over the country and from people at various football clubs. I was very grateful to them all for their kindness. But this was different.

The nurses came rushing in thinking that I had had some sort of failure.

The staff and other patients in the hospital already knew I was a rabid fan of Everton, because I had been

Rooney receives treatment off the pitch for his suspected broken foot during the Euro 2004 quarter final against Portugal.

boring everybody to death about Wayne Rooney. I had returned just a month earlier from covering the Euro 2004 championships in Portugal, where, for me and many others, the Everton teenager had been the player of the tournament.

Most of the doctors and nurses who were interested in football agreed with me and I had already told the story over and over again about how I had witnessed first-hand his amazing performances for his country until his broken metatarsal put paid to his tournament – and probably England's chances of winning it.

The nurses asked me what was wrong. Having lost the power of speech I just pointed at the shirt.

His signature was the very distinctive right-leaning moniker with a big 'W', a big 'R' and a big 'Y'. Completely stunned, I said, 'Wayne Rooney has just sent me a signed shirt.'

The nurses realised the scale of my wonderment and started running up and down the corridor to tell everybody.

To appreciate the moment fully, I have to put into perspective the atmosphere prevailing in the country at the time.

The whole of England was deliriously in love with the boy wonder who, during the course of the previous month, had gone from being a cheeky little Scouser on the fringes of the England team to the most talked-about boy in Britain.

His football had been exhilarating, scoring four goals in two games and winning us a penalty against France. He had cut a tragic but sympathetic figure as he sat on the grass in the Stadium of Light in Lisbon, as his broken foot was being diagnosed. It was the end of England's ambitions in Portugal, but the start of the Rooney worldwide legend.

'I don't remember anyone making such an impact on a tournament since Pele in the 1958 World Cup in Sweden.'

Sven-Goran Eriksson, after Euro 2004

At that stage, he didn't have a single detractor. He played for Everton, who are not a club that provokes any great hostility, and people were still chuckling over the stories about him playing in the Premiership one moment and having a kick-about with his mates in the street a few hours later, as he had done for years.

> **Rooney has a tattoo at the base of his spine which reads 'Then'. It was his first, done as a lark with a mate, who has one at the base of his spine which reads 'OK'. The duo were constantly ribbed for being inseparable and ending every sentence with 'OK, then.' Each had one word inscribed to have the last laugh.**

If we are to believe everything we read, then he would turn up for training with Everton on his mountain bike and have double sausage, chips and beans for his tea every night.

He was a raw Scouse kid who had taken on some of the world's best players in an England shirt and made us all proud of the fact that he was one of ours.

People had been transfixed by his performances in

Portugal. Football fans loved him for his genius, mothers loved him because he could have been their little lad and millions of us had stood in bars and even on street corners throughout the summer to see the legend unfold.

He had become an untouchable colossus, in the same sort of way that you would think about Paul McCartney or Muhammad Ali – you didn't believe that you were made of the same flesh and bone as they are. Rooney had moved to that sort of iconic status.

I could not have been more chuffed to receive that shirt. Well, if he could have fixed my heart that might have just been better, but, realistically, I was in a state of happy shock.

A nurse was hugging me. She kept repeating, 'Wayne Rooney in our hospital ... I can't believe it.'

He wasn't there, of course, but he might as well have been for the excitement it was generating. It was true hero-worship.

And now I was a hero, too. The nurses figured that if I hadn't been a patient at Harefield then there wouldn't be a Wayne Rooney signed shirt next to my bed. People came around all day to see it. Talk about reflected glory!

In those first few moments as the nurse was embracing me, I felt tears rolling down my cheeks. I wasn't consciously crying, but the past few weeks had been miserable and desperate.

I had been haunted by the look of pain and helplessness on my mother's face when she had last come to see me and realised just how ill I was. The Rooney shirt just made me feel fantastic.

When you are very ill, you are fighting a mental as

well as a physical battle. The doctors had already been happy with my positive outlook. I was badgering them for a transplant as though they could suddenly take a new heart off a supermarket shelf.

I wanted them to know that I didn't fear the future. Some patients have such a tough time that when that dramatic moment comes and you're told that there is potentially a donor heart available, some patients panic like mad and can't go through with it. But the arrival of the Rooney shirt had been a tremendous lift for me.

Life had been looking very grey, but suddenly it had become a kaleidoscope of colour again: it shook me out of what was becoming a depression and gave me renewed hope for the future. It undoubtedly kick-started a sense of renewed resistance in me, which I believe eventually led to me being able to control my illness with drugs, as I do today, and to avoid the need for a transplant.

Though that moment remains unforgettable for me, Wayne Rooney had already played a telling part in my arrival back in England before I had become desperately – almost critically – ill.

England went out of Euro 2004 because Wayne Rooney broke his foot. I didn't want that and he certainly didn't want that, but the fact that he had cracked his metatarsal had a major bearing on my future.

Whatever happened in Portugal, I was going to stay there as long as England were on course to win the competition. I had no idea how ill I was as my heart deteriorated during the course of the competition.

I had been to see a number of doctors prior to going to the European Championships, but none of them had diagnosed the real problem. I had been told several times that I had a chest infection. One Australian doctor, on duty in casualty on a bank holiday, told me to stop imagining things and assured me that the funny noises coming up my throat were perfectly normal.

In the second game of the championships in Portugal, England played Switzerland in a little town called Coimbra, 100 miles north of Lisbon. The temperature in the football ground was 100 degrees Fahrenheit and, as the stadium had only just about been completed in time for the game, it was very dusty.

There was not even a roof over our seats and I felt terribly uncomfortable. When the players came out to exercise half an hour before the game, Rooney was the closest England player to me and was bouncing around like a rubber band. I started thinking to myself, 'I know that I shouldn't be able to move around the way Rooney does, but these days I can hardly move at all.'

Because of the pace of the tournament, and the fact that I was getting up at 4.30am every morning to do the breakfast show on talkSPORT with Alan Brazil and then chasing around all over Portugal, I had not really noticed that I was physically grinding to a halt.

Usually when you are away, you can put that down to successive nights on the drink with a gang of other hacks, but because of the heat, and the fact that I was the boss of the ten-strong talkSPORT team, I had decided not to drink at all in Portugal.

I thought it would be a tough vow to keep, but it

turned out to be rather easy. I didn't even feel like a drink and that, in itself, was odd for me.

After the game, which England won with ease with Rooney scoring twice, I wanted to make a quick getaway to get back to Lisbon for the following day's breakfast show and I was intending to do a runner a few minutes before the end with England safely leading by three goals. But the minute I tried to start running, I nearly collapsed. I couldn't get any air into my lungs and I was lying flat out on a pavement outside the stadium, absolutely gasping for breath.

Fortunately, I was able to contact my producer Jim Brown on the mobile phone. Jim, a fitness fanatic and a body-builder, got our truck close enough to the stadium to be able to come and physically pick me up off the street and get me home. Sadly, Jim is no longer with us.

I couldn't sleep that night. Every time I closed my eyes, everything started spinning around and it felt as though I was drowning.

At that stage, the most sensible thing to have done would have been to return home, but there was no way I was leaving Portugal while England were still in the competition. We had a great chance to win it. In addition, I had been beating the Rooney drum for weeks ahead of the tournament in the column I wrote for a group of regional evening newspapers owned by Trinity Mirror. They had titles in most of the nation's footballing hotspots, like Liverpool, Newcastle and Birmingham.

I had warned their readers to watch England's secret weapon – Wayne Rooney. The readers of the papers outside of Liverpool, and even half of that city itself, sent hundreds of letters to the sports editors saying that

I had gone mad and that Rooney would be chewed up and spat out. Now that I was being proved right, I was determined to stick with it.

For the next four days I could only just drag myself out of bed, do the breakfast show and then retire again.

England played Croatia back in Lisbon and we won again with another Rooney double. We had reached the quarter-finals, but in the three days leading up to that game I was deteriorating rapidly.

We were beaten on penalties in the Stadium of Light against Portugal after Rooney had been sidelined with his broken foot.

I was devastated. I honestly thought we were going to win the tournament. The only slight compensation for me was that now we were out, I could go home.

If Rooney had not broken his foot and if England had not gone out, I would have stayed. Doctors have since told me that there was a very good chance that had I stayed, I would have killed myself.

We packed up the day after England's exit and were due to fly back the following morning. The boys were all having a leaving party and, not wanting to be a killjoy, I decided to join them and have a drink for the first time. I summoned my last reserves of strength and went down to the bar to dispense with vast quantities of drink.

For some reason, I could not drink anything alcoholic except Baileys; wine tasted like vinegar and beer just wouldn't go down my throat. But as the Baileys disappeared down the hatch, I felt better than I had done for the last three weeks. I suddenly thought that whatever was wrong with me was all in my mind.

Until the next day, that is. I was so ill that I couldn't stand up straight without fainting. I now started to worry that something was really wrong.

I'm sure there are very good medical facilities in Portugal but, at times like this, you just want to get home. You want to be in an English hospital. But I was frightened ... I wasn't even sure that I was going to make it home.

I somehow got to the airport, but couldn't carry any bags, including my pride and joy set of Calloway golf clubs. I didn't have the strength. If I had been running the airline that brought me back, I would not have let me on the plane. I was sweating profusely and couldn't make it up the steps without help.

When a car picked me up at Heathrow, I was delirious. I should have gone straight to a hospital, but I just wanted to go to bed. I was crawling under the duvet even before my driver had finished bringing in my luggage.

I tried to pretend to everybody that I was okay, because it was the weekend and I didn't want any fuss. On Monday morning, I got a car to take me to the doctor's surgery.

As soon as the receptionist saw me, she fast-tracked me into a surgery where a very efficient GP suspected that something was wrong with my heart.

Within an hour, I was in the consulting rooms of a top cardiologist, who told me later that he knew I was in trouble the minute I walked in. Apparently, my veins were bulging unnaturally and, when he lifted my trouser legs, he found my ankles horribly swollen.

When your heart begins to pack up, it no longer pushes the fluids around your body in the way it should.

Gravity takes over and that is why your ankles swell up and also, when you lie down, you think you are drowning because fluid pours into your lungs.

Acute heart failure was diagnosed within minutes. I was rushed off to hospital and pints of water were drained from my body. The specialist told me later that my condition was so serious that he could not have been certain that I would have survived that night if I had not been treated when I was.

I don't want to be melodramatic, but if England had still been in Euro 2004, I would have stayed to watch the rest of the tournament. Or would I? Who knows?

All I do know is that the reason I came home when I did was because England had been knocked out. And it is universally accepted that we went out because Wayne Rooney broke his foot.

But there I was in hospital and, as a result of a tremendous act of kindness by Rooney, I felt better than I had done for the previous two months.

The psychological lift was staggering. I don't think people in Rooney's position can ever understand how they can affect people's lives for the better.

I was already well aware of the compassionate side of the Croxteth Kid. He had made his entry into top-flight football in the most dramatic fashion with a stunning goal against Arsenal's David Seaman in October 2002, and anybody who was more self-aware would have taken their boots home that day and maybe given them to his parents – or perhaps just kept them as a souvenir and had them put into a glass case. But not Rooney: he gave them to a specialist childrens' hospital, a world-renowned institution where his girlfriend Coleen's disabled sister had been receiving treatment. They were auctioned to raise funds.

Even more astonishing was his decision to give away his first ever England shirt for charity. Fortunately, I now own it.

This is the red shirt he wore against Australia in the match at Upton Park on 12 February 2003. I remember it as a bitterly cold night and I wasn't really interested in the first half, because Sven-Goran Eriksson had fielded the expected England side.

I wanted to be there if and when he changed the team around for the second half to give Rooney his first cap. If he did, it was going to be an historical night.

Sure enough, in the second half, Sven put out a whole new team of substitutes and there, leading the England attack, was Wayne Rooney of Everton

At seventeen years and 111 days he became the youngest ever England player. He was accompanied up front by Francis Jeffers, himself a former Everton player.

England's patchwork team lost 3-1 that night, but the scoreline was irrelevant. Rooney would go down in the record books for ever more. He was an Everton player and, as far as I was concerned, another attachment had been added to the rich tradition of that club.

A year later, I got a call from a chap called Stuart Silk. Stu was the charity manager of RMCC, Ronald McDonald Children's Charities, an organisation that helps parents who had desperately ill children.

If a child had to be transferred to a specialist hospital miles away from home, the parents often found themselves unable to be with their little one because of the prohibitive cost of accommodation. This could be a particular problem in big cities like London where, for instance, many children are taken to Guy's Hospital for specialist heart treatment. RMCC build accommodation blocks where the parents can stay for free and where they are often able to have their children with them.

Rooney's agents had sorted out a deal between their boy and McDonald's, the parent organisation of RMCC, who are a big sponsor throughout football. When Wayne learned of the charity, amazingly he gave them his first England shirt.

It was a staggering gesture. Not only was it *his* first English shirt it was *the* England shirt worn by the player who had made history by becoming the youngest ever to represent his country. It's the sort of artefact that you might imagine seeing in the Football Association's museum in 100 years time. In football terms, it's a national treasure.

Stuart Silk had rung me as a regular listener to the talkSPORT breakfast show, because he knew I was a big Rooney fan. He told me that the shirt was going to be put up for auction at a forthcoming sportsmen's dinner in London and, as it was his job to maximise fundraising, he wanted to know if I had any interest in coming along to bid.

I was delighted that he had got in touch, but I had two problems. Firstly, I was going to be out of town on the night of the dinner, hosting a fan's forum with Alan Brazil. And, secondly, I couldn't believe that I, a humble radio presenter, would be in the league of some of the big shots you see at these dinners who think nothing of

Everton old-boy and Academy team-mate Francis Jeffers congratulates Rooney on a debut job well done.

paying £10,000 for a pair of boxer's gloves that they don't even want.

Stuart said that he would find a bidder for me, though I told him that I thought it was probably going to be out of my league and that I could only afford to go up to £2,500. I knew I had no hope of acquiring the shirt, but on the night of the auction I became annoyed with myself for having been so miserable with my budget. I wanted to double it, but I couldn't get hold of Stu.

I was working that night and again on the breakfast show the following morning in Glasgow. I didn't get back to London until the following morning and I checked my e-mails. I couldn't believe it when I saw a message telling me that I had acquired the shirt. I had outbid everybody else at £1,500. I can only assume that the significance of what was on offer did not register with most people.

I went over to the RMCC home at Guy's Hospital to pick up my shirt. It was framed; it had the details of the game stitched on the front, England vs Australia, 12 February 2003, a big, bold white No. 23 and the Three Lions emblem. Across the top of the number is written: 'Best Wishes, Wayne Rooney.'

I was very moved by the work that the charity's homes were doing. There was one young couple there from northern England who were petrified by their little baby's heart illness and who could not possibly have afforded to stay in London on their own.

Stuart Silk, talking about fundraising, said, 'We are a pretty unknown charity, so having a Wayne Rooney association is quite incredible. It has given us a profile that we could not possibly have hoped for on a day-to-day basis ... He's been tremendously generous and interested in what we do. We've had boots from him as well as the shirt. The effect is incalculable.'

I was terrified about taking the shirt home in case I got mugged. Alan Brazil had come with me to the hospital to say hello to a few people, because his little girl, Steffie, had been treated there as a baby.

On the way back, we stopped in a wine bar in Fleet Street, but I was too nervous to drink. I had visions of getting drunk and leaving the bar without my shirt. I walked out into the street, hailed a cab and went straight home. Today, the shirt is in a walk-in safe in a solicitor's office, because it has become such a constant source of interest.

Within a few months, Rooney was lighting up the stage in Portugal and had become a world famous footballer and I've often wondered what that shirt would have cost me four months after Euro 2004, rather than four months before it.

In the months after the competition, I found myself in hospital and the recipient of his get-well-soon shirt. It may just be a coincidence, but I started on the long road to recovery from that moment. I firmly believe that the two are connected.

Over the next few months, I started responding to drugs that had previously made me terribly ill. My appetite gradually came back and soon I was able to walk outside again.

When I was in hospital, I was sometimes allowed home at weekends, but I had had to stay at my sister's, because I didn't have the puff to get up the stairs to my own top-floor flat.

I slowly regained the strength to climb stairs and

started to get home more and more often. One day, I even managed to walk to the post box, which is about 70 yards down the road. It was a major victory and I couldn't stop smiling all day.

The doctors assessed me and decided to take me off the transplant list. Today, I enjoy a remarkable level of normality. I take a large combination of drugs each day and they keep me pretty stable. I go to work and, apart from very strenuous activity, I do what most other people can do.

It's not certain how I recovered after having been so ill. I have regular check-ups and the function of my heart has technically not improved from the days when I was bed-ridden. But doctors and nurses worked tirelessly to find the pills and tablets that would combine best to keep me going. Those drugs drain my body of water, fortify my heart, thin my blood so that it doesn't clot, and give me the strength to move around. I can't thank the medical team enough.

But I also believe that Wayne Rooney had a lot to do with it.

TWO

BLUE GOD TO RED DEVIL?

THE BOY STOOD, hands in pockets, staring unflinchingly at Bill Kenwright, the chairman of Everton football club. He was no more than thirteen years old, but already the blue blood of 'The Toffees' ran through his veins.

Kenwright had parked his car 400 yards away and strolled, as he usually did, along Goodison Road, meeting and greeting fans before the team's match, on this occasion against Blackburn.

I watched, as ever, while he clearly enjoyed a bit of banter with the club's faithful fans before the game. It was something I'd seen him do a hundred times before and it was part of the theatre of match day on Merseyside.

The fans loved him for it: for being one of them – a man whose passion for Everton had led him to take the incredible gamble of investing everything he had in acquiring his beloved football club.

It's not like he needed to. Kenwright was already

world famous as one of the most successful theatre impresarios on both sides of the Atlantic, a man who had been responsible for some of the biggest West End and Broadway productions.

He must be used to big audiences, but even among this modest array of cheerful fans, there was one boy who stood out. He was an angelic-looking youngster, who bristled with a calm confidence and intent as he walked up to Kenwright.

'Why aren't you playing Rooney?' he fired at the chairman without preamble.

Kenwright was flummoxed. Wayne Rooney was becoming very well known to Everton fans, but he hadn't even arrived in the first-team squad yet and had certainly never been heard of on the back pages of the newspapers.

A little taken aback, Kenwright replied: 'I don't pick the team, son.'

The boy, unfazed, fired off another question, as the crowd became intrigued at the cheek of the youngster cross-examining Everton's saviour.

'I know,' the boy persisted, 'but why isn't Moyesy playing Rooney then?'

'Well,' said Kenwright, clearly on the back foot. 'He's not sixteen yet.'

The boy wasn't going to give up. Doggedly, he insisted, 'Yes he is, he's had his birthday.'

'Oh, well, yes, but he hasn't left school yet,' said Kenwright, intrigued by the boy's evident passion and knowledge of Everton's secret weapon.

'Yes he has,' the boy confidently shot back. 'He left yesterday.'

A smile spread across Kenwright's face as he warmed to his interrogator. 'Who are you?' he asked, with a dawn of recognition suddenly appearing behind his trademark black-rimmed glasses. 'How do you know?'

'Because I'm his brother,' replied the boy, Graham. 'And you should be playing our Wayne.'

It was evidence, if evidence were ever needed, that the Rooney clan had one goal: to see their boy turn out

Wayne's younger brother and constant champion, Graham, in action on the pitch.

in the colours of the club that was a religion within their family.

They worshipped at the altar of Goodison Park and their terraced house on the tough Croxteth council estate was impossible to miss because of the Everton pennants that adorned its windows.

Those who witnessed the conversation could have had no idea that they were watching the start of a phenomenon that would, within five years, sweep not only the country but the world.

Everton Chairman Bill Kenwright, centre, looking out over his beloved Goodison Park.

I heard another fan, who was watching as Graham confronted the chairman, say to his mate, 'They're talking about Wayne Rooney. That's his brother.'

'Yeah,' Graham piped up as he turned to the two men in front of me, 'He is my brother and he's gonna be the best player in the world.'

At every Premiership football club, you'll hear devoted fans talk about an up-and-coming youngster who is going to be 'the greatest'. Most of the time it's wishful thinking, to say the least, and when you look at the records, it is almost improbable that any club will produce one player in a generation who will even go on to play for England.

But the way the boy was talking, and the clear recognition he was getting from the chairman, gave everybody who witnessed the exchange the feeling that this was not just another awestruck fan. Kenwright, a little flustered, did his usual two-handed wave to the faithful before entering the hallowed ground.

To many, this was the first indication that the boy Rooney, whose name was already whispered with reverence in the bars around Goodison, was a level above the rest of the youngsters who are churned out on the youth academy production line. Before that confrontation in the street, it is unlikely that anyone had ever witnessed the chairman of a football club being interrogated by a schoolboy about a player who, up to that point, had not even had his name in the programme. However, within a few months, the name of Rooney was spreading like a bushfire across Merseyside.

For years, he had been playing for Everton teams, from schoolboy to youth, creating goal-scoring records along the way. Among those who knew, tales of his brilliance were becoming routine.

> **Wayne's talent as a young lad was prodigious; he scored 99 goals in just one season for Everton Youth Under-10s.**

On that day, as I was standing outside Goodison Park, I sensed the strangest sort of feeling that there was something in the atmosphere that I had never experienced before.

As word spread up and down the street about the verbal joust between Kenwright and 'the kid brother', the tales of Rooney's prowess as a footballer grew and grew. In each story, he was judged to be better than the last. He was a magician with electric feet, then the white Pelé and, ultimately, a messiah.

Suddenly, I believed that I had witnessed the start of a new, intriguing chapter in the glorious history of Everton Football Club. Some kind of revolution was about to happen and Rooney would be the dynamite to ignite it.

I stood there in wonderment at what I had just witnessed, taking in the atmosphere that runs up and down the streets of terraced housing in the hours before a game. But what I could never have possibly imagined was that, within a few years, I'd be sharing a beer with Wayne Rooney – no, not the boy himself, but his dad – in a pub, 10 yards behind where I stood. And we wouldn't be celebrating another vintage performance by the youngest England player of all time. Instead, we would both be drowning our sorrows that the greatest footballer of his generation no longer played for his beloved Everton and, probably, that he would never pull on the famous blue shirt again.

The boy who had become a saviour to a great club in the doldrums would now be viewed by many on Merseyside as a Judas. He had become the most expensive footballing teenager in the world by joining Manchester United.

On the day I first witnessed Rooney fever at Goodison, I would never have believed it possible if anybody had told me that he would leave his beloved club after asking for a transfer.

This was the subject occupying Wayne Rooney Sr and I as we supped pints of bitter in The Winslow, a diehard Everton fans' pub that is literally in the shadow of the main stand at Goodison Park.

That night, the Rooney lad had scored twice for his new club, 35 miles away in Manchester. It had brought into focus the enormous dilemma of the Rooney family, who still supported Everton, while the boy himself was creating a worldwide reputation in a Red Devil's shirt.

Wayne Sr had just watched Everton lose 2-1 to West Ham to perpetuate their poor start to the season. In contrast, his son had taken the honours once again as he was the two-goal hero and Man of the Match in a 4-0 victory over Wigan that kept United hot on the heels of Chelsea in their quest for an amazing ninth Premiership trophy in fourteen years.

Clearly, this torturous dilemma was causing the father at the head of a true-blue Everton family a lot of heartache. During the course of a great after-match session, it became clear that he was torn between the normal loyalties a father has to his son and the club that had been supported by the whole of his family for all of their lives. And let's face it, Wayne Rooney is no ordinary son when it comes to loyalties.

I expect him to be acknowledged as the greatest footballer in the world. But his father cannot commit to becoming a Manchester United devotee.

When his son first returned to Goodison Park in a red shirt after United had drawn Everton in the fifth round of the FA Cup, it became a nightmare for the Rooney family.

By that time, Wayne Sr and his wife Jeanette were allowed the use of a box at Goodison Park due to the obvious attention they attracted every week because of who they are. But even in the privacy of that enclosed environment, the parents did not feel that it was right to put themselves in a position that would test their dual loyalties.

> **His dad, Wayne Sr, is a pigeon fancier – and gets on famously with Wayne's boyhood hero and Everton star Duncan Ferguson, who shares his passion, and keeps a loft of 25 pigeons at his £1.2 million mansion.**

Of course, they want their boy to be a star every time he takes to a football field but, at the same time, they want Everton to win every game they play.

They must have been asked a million times in the weeks leading up to the game, 'Who do you want to win?' They never answered the question, because they were in the ultimate no-win situation.

Father, Wayne Sr, mother Jeanette and brother Graham watch the tense action at Euro 2004, some weeks before Wayne Jr's eventful transfer.

They finally decided not to accept the offer of hospitality on the day of the game and, because of their unique circumstances, have never commented on the outcome of it.

Their decision not to go to the game turned out to be a wise one, because more than one fan was spotted in the ground wearing a shirt bearing the slogan, 'We hate him so much because we loved him so much.'

What father would want to subject his wife to having to witness that sort of behaviour, knowing that the bile was aimed at their son?

Rooney Sr understands why so many people in the

city were devastated by his lad's departure to their arch-rivals along the M62. And, naturally, he would have preferred his son to have spent a glorious career regenerating Everton and becoming a legend alongside the likes of Dixie Dean, Brian Labone and Alex Young in the history of the club that was founded in 1878. But, nevertheless, he feels the strain of the continuing debate about whether Wayne was justified in pursuing his ambition or whether he abandoned the club he clearly adored when they badly needed him.

Part of the community in which he is immersed, and in which he has been all of his life, turned against his boy. It only took a few hours after the transfer had officially been completed for the graffiti merchants to get to work on the walls of Goodison Park: 'Could Have Been a God – But Chose to be a Devil' was the mildest of the form of angry words painted in white beneath the Everton crest.

Another fan had scrawled 'Rooney – Judas'. Across the road, on the walls of Gladwys Street Primary School, was the less restrained 'Die Rooney Die', this time sprayed in black.

In one sense, since those angry slogans appeared, the issue has been flattened by the fact that, following Rooney's departure, Everton, who were one of the favourites for relegation without him, had their best ever season in the Premiership.

Amazingly, they qualified for the Champions League, a feat so remarkable that David Moyes was voted Manager of the Year, even above Jose Mourinho, 'the special one', who had brought Chelsea their first title for fifty years. In addition, nearly £25 million eventually flowed into the empty Everton coffers and, within two years, they were twentieth in the list of the world's richest football clubs.

But for some – including Bill Kenwright – the pain of Rooney's departure remains unbearable, despite the financial compensations.

Many hoped that the alternative equation would work: by staying at Everton on a deal that would have given him £50,000 a week, at eighteen years of age, it would have attracted other great players to the club and thus generate an era of success to put Everton back among the very best. This theory will never be tested.

Although Rooney was a fervent Evertonian, to the extent that he once went to a Liverpool trial as a schoolboy wearing a blue shirt, he is also ruthlessly ambitious. After weeks of speculation following his explosion onto the world stage at Euro 2004, Rooney resolved to take control of his own destiny.

Against Merseysiders' worries about possible manipulation of the 'impressionable' youngster, Rooney proved to have a ruthless life focus. Nothing impresses him unduly, and he simply can't be manipulated.

Those who have grown up with him know that he was born with the maturity of a man in his mid-twenties and, when he sets his mind on something, like dating Coleen McLoughlin or just getting a new mountain bike, he usually gets what he wants.

His agent, Paul Stretford, is very much a man of the same ilk. Spotting the enormous potential in Rooney, he entered into a round of business battles and court cases to acquire Wayne as his own. He's even found himself battered in a courtroom in his determination that he will

Wayne's agent Paul
Stretford, seen here at a
charity golf tournament
in Portugal.

be to the footballer what Brian Epstein was to that other great Merseyside phenomenon, The Beatles, at the height of their fame and popularity.

One of the reasons why there was such an explosive response to the transfer across the whole of the city of Liverpool was because of the way that matters spiralled to a head in the last forty-eight hours of August 2004.

Wayne was able to keep his head down as speculation, claim, counter-claim and newspaper headline wrapped themselves together in a fog of unreliable informaton. Because he had broken his metatarsal in the quarter-final game against Portugal in Lisbon, he was not training with Everton and was, therefore, not in the public eye. But if he had been fit, he has said that he would have played for Everton, no matter what the reaction of the crowd had been in the midst of all the speculation: it was still his club until any decision had been made for him to go anywhere else.

As the transfer window at the start of the 2004-05 season was drawing to a close, Everton believed that they had done enough to persuade their protégé to stay with the club he adored. However, there were undoubtedly some faint hearts both in and around Goodison. For those who didn't have blue blood coursing through their veins like Kenwright, Rooney was seen as a cash-cow. Everton were struggling with debt and the value of footballers can fluctuate notoriously, depending on their form and their physical fitness.

If Everton were to get relegated the following season, as everybody was predicting, then they would have been forced to sell their prime asset in a fire-sale. On the back of the worldwide impression he had made at Euro 2004, Rooney was at his premium worth right then.

Bill Kenwright, the businessman, was well aware of that, but instead of bowing to those who believed that the time was right to sell, he turned the argument against them and declared that the price for Rooney was £100 million pounds and not a penny less. Kenwright was being theatrically fanciful, but he realistically believed that Rooney was worth £50 million – which he probably is today – and that Everton shouldn't even consider selling him for any less.

Manager David Moyes was firing the same sort of salvos when he repeatedly said that Rooney could only go for a record figure.

'We don't want to lose Wayne,' he said defiantly. 'But if we do, the only way is at the top price and the value we want ... Didier Drogba went to Chelsea for £24 million, so Wayne's price should be a lot more than that.'

Despite all this resistance, hearts were broken, from the boardroom at Goodison Park to supporters' clubs all over the world when, with forty-eight hours to go, Kenwright took a call on his mobile phone. The very distinctive voice of Wayne Rooney was on the other end. He was distressed.

Sobbing, Wayne told Kenwright, 'I'm sorry Mr Chairman, I've got to go.'

In a fleeting moment, Wayne's future had been decided.

A few minutes later, David Moyes received a similar call from the emotional young man, stating the same message: 'I'm sorry boss, I've got to go.'

Rooney couldn't even get out the words to tell either Kenwright or Moyes that he was destined for Manchester United.

A shattered Kenwright, who was devastated by the sharp turn of events, said, 'When I got the call I knew that things were moving on and there was almost nothing I could do about it. Nothing ... It was obvious what a tough decision it was for Wayne to say that he wanted to leave and, although it went against every grain of Blue in my body, I had to try and understand why he had made that decision ... It was the worst summer of my life. No one felt more pain than I did about Wayne going.'

And in a deeply philosophical mood the day after the transfer was concluded, he added, 'Wayne is simply the best prospect I have ever seen in an Everton shirt. The lad said in his press conference after signing for Manchester United that the transfer was probably much delayed because of the tremendous efforts Everton made to keep him and he is absolutely right.

'David Moyes and I had many meetings, both together and separately, with Wayne's advisers, and on several occasions we both felt that we were pretty close to an agreement that would keep him at the club. However, literally days before the August transfer window closed, it became very clear from Wayne that he really did want to leave Everton and, unfortunately, by that stage, David and I found that we had no option but to let him go.'

A few days later, the chairman received a personal note from Wayne thanking him for all he had done for him at Everton and expressing his regret at moving on; he also stated that he felt he had to make the tough decision at that stage of his career.

Kenwright said, 'It didn't really surprise me, because that was the sort of lad he has always been.

Nevertheless, considering everything that had gone on in such a short space of time, and all the hassle surrounding the transfer, it was nice to know he was still thinking about us.'

To this day, Kenwright still cannot bear to watch Wayne play in a Manchester United shirt.

The chairman is a very close business confidant of Lord Andrew Lloyd-Webber, the world's top theatre man, and is a personal friend of Phillip Green, the BHS high street magnate. But the person who was having such a devastating effect on his life was a teenager from the sort of background that was the polar opposite of that elite circle of friends.

I remember once being in the directors' lounge at Goodison, having a chat with Kenwright after what was only young Rooney's sixth senior game and I said to him, 'What are you going to do when he becomes a legend here, Bill?'

Quick as a flash he hit back, saying, 'What do you mean when? Are you blind?' Such was Kenwright's adoration of his young footballer.

But from the moment he took the phone call signalling the end of Rooney's career at Everton, the practicality had to take over to allow the club to drive the hardest bargain for a player they knew was going to be a world-beater. Massive disappointment had to be put on hold while the telephone lines between Merseyside and Manchester buzzed as detailed negotiations took place about a transfer that was about to rock the footballing world.

It was never certain until the last moment that Rooney would go to Manchester United. In fact, Newcastle

United started the transfer scramble by putting in an opening bid of a staggering £23 million. It was also rumoured that Chelsea might swoop at the last minute to gazump any earlier bid, aided by the seemingly endless supply of money in the pockets Russian billionaire Roman Abramovich.

Once Rooney had decided to go, however, there was little doubt that Manchester United were the favourites to add him to their squad. He had mixed with United players in the England squad in Portugal and he yearned to be part of an organisation that felt as big and as successful as the Mancunian superclub.

Also, with his family connections, and those of girlfriend Coleen McLoughlin, it is safe to say he didn't want to travel too far away from his Merseyside roots; far enough to avoid the animosity he knew was coming his way, but not so far that he couldn't keep in touch with the community in which he had grown up.

Within twenty-four hours of the announcement that Rooney wanted to leave Everton, it became obvious that Manchester United was indeed going to be Rooney's new club. Another twenty-four hours later, on Tuesday 21 August 2004, the transfer was complete.

Nobody could have predicted the sort of anti-Rooney fall-out that erupted after pictures of Rooney in his Dennis the Menace jumper appeared on television sets all over the country as he arrived at Old Trafford. In addition to the graffiti on the walls around Goodison Park, outraged fans started to bombard local radio stations.

There were reports of crazy death threats to the footballer and his agent. One group of fans even advocated that the whole crowd at the next Everton home game should get up and leave the ground en masse as a protest – though it was never clear as to whom that protest was specifically going to be aimed at.

It was impossible for thousands of lifelong Evertonians to understand how Rooney could have gone. As with many communities that surround a lot of traditional clubs in diehard areas, football in the blue

area of Liverpool is actually the most important aspect of many people's lives. It was a mystery to many how a young lad who had achieved the impossible dream of moving from the terraces to the pitch could suddenly give up his Everton fairy-tale.

To a lot of them, the definition of Rooney as an Evertonian came when he was pictured in a shirt that

Happier times for Rooney at Everton, seen here on the bench.

had the following words written on it: 'Once a Blue, always a Blue.'

He wore it on a t-shirt under his royal blue Everton strip and flashed it to his adoring crowd after scoring against Aston Villa in the final of the FA Youth Cup at Goodison Park.

There were two points of view. The first was unequivocal: Rooney was a traitor. The second, put forward by a largely silent body of fans, was: 'What would you have done in his shoes?'

Derek Hatton, the former firebrand deputy leader of Liverpool City Council and a lifelong Everton fan, reacted to the move by saying, 'If you were his dad, what would you have told him to do?'

This was an ironic view of the situation, because Wayne Rooney Sr had actually played no part at all in his son's transfer. He had simply been caught up in the maelstrom.

And it was within yards from where the graffiti had appeared on the walls around Goodison that I was last having that beer with Wayne Sr after he had chosen to watch Everton rather than his own son.

Old Trafford is only forty minutes away by car, but Rooney Sr didn't see the latest two goals his son had scored for United until he got home later that night.

'I was keeping track of what was going on by reading what was in the papers,' he said.

Reluctant to be sucked into the still-talked-about transfer saga, he would only add, 'It's not very nice to see abusive messages about your lad sprayed on walls across his home city.'

Though the Rooney family had hoped that their lives

would not change to any significant degree, it soon became impossible for them not to be affected by the worldwide interest being taken in their son.

Even before Wayne left Everton, they had been forced to move house because, as Rooney Sr said to one neighbour, 'How many times can you put up with somebody knocking on your door day and night?'

Unfortunately, it wasn't just people knocking on the door: it was malcontents causing trouble and damage to the Rooney family home and their cars.

The most famous father in Britain remains determined to stay out of the debate about his son and Everton. He knows that the first time he gets sucked into any sort of a discussion, he will find himself in a classic situation where whatever he says will have been the wrong thing to have said. He doesn't want to hear people's opinions, so he doesn't put himself in a position where he will hear them.

Ideally, he wants to continue with his life supporting Everton Football Club with as little fuss as possible, while at the same time showing a proud and caring interest in his son's career – just as any father would. To that extent, he surrounds himself with his old mates who have been going to the football with him for years. He drinks with a close group of muckers, he keeps a very low profile and, by doing it that way, he cuts down the chances of being hassled.

The transfer saga had come less than 100 weeks after Wayne had exploded onto the soccer scene with the goal that led Arsenal manager Arsène Wenger to describe him as the finest young talent in English football.

But the speculation had begun even before that. From the start of 2004, there had been a persistent buzz around football, and in Liverpool in particular, that Rooney was going to Manchester United.

A lot of it was probably the mischievous mutterings of Liverpool fans and the logical expectancy that a good performance from Wayne at Euro 2004 would open up the inevitable debate.

As early as the day after the 2004 FA Cup final, in which Manchester United beat Millwall 3-0, the *Sunday People* had reported exclusively that a deal with Sir Alex Ferguson, United's manager, was about to be done.

I wasn't the only person – Bill Kenwright said he was told as much a dozen times himself – to be told by a taxi driver, claiming to be Rooney's uncle in their extended family, that, 'Our Wayne is going to Man United – the deal is done.'

However, there's no evidence that any deal was 'done' or that Wayne had even taken part in any discussions about his future at that stage. There did, however, seem to be a general belief by a pocket of people in the city that Wayne was going to be transferred to a much bigger club in the summer and when the anticipated, but feared, transfer race got underway, the starting gun was fired in an unlikely location ... it was Newcastle United who made the first bid.

It's not really clear why they decided to involve themselves – apart from the fact that Rooney is a brilliant player – because nobody ever really believed that Rooney was going to go to the North-East.

This did not really fit the objective of this painful

exercise: Rooney wanted to move to 'a higher level of football'. Newcastle are certainly a very big club with gates that are second only to Manchester United, but their Champions League record is unspectacular and they haven't picked up any domestic silverware for fifty years.

It is hard to know what sort of response Wayne Rooney thought he would get from the Everton fans who saw him as the Second Coming, the boy prodigy who was going to open up a golden new era for the club. Some of his advisers had told him that he wouldn't have a problem; that he would always be regarded as an Evertonian and that, as he was spawned within an Evertonian community, he would always be regarded as one of them. Others tried to tell him that, far from being seen as any sort of a traitor, he would in fact be hailed as a saviour, because his transfer was going to bring in tens of millions of pounds and that he was single-handedly going to save Everton Football Club. What greater gift could he make to Evertonians?

But it was through the middle of this that Rooney's true character emerged. He revealed a rod of steel down his backbone.

Initially, he was clearly distressed at having had to make the decision that would take him away from the club that had formed the focal part of his life during his illustrious schoolboy football career. The genuine tears to chairman Kenwright and manager Moyes proved that to be the case.

But rather rapidly, as the confirmation of the transfer deal became public, the mood around Goodison Park changed ... and so did that of the young footballer.

By the time Everton played West Bromwich Albion at

home on Saturday 28 August, only their third game of the new season, a profound sense of shock had set in across the blue half of Merseyside.

The transfer deal was in active negotiation. Everton were holding out for between £30–40 million, but United wanted a staged deal involving bonus payments for appearances and the possibility of players in exchange.

While all this was going on behind the scenes, the public face of the Rooney transfer began to take a very nasty turn. Banners had been hastily put together by fans who displayed them during the West Brom game with venomous slogans like 'Judas'. The graffiti artists had already started their work on the walls outside.

The young footballer had not really known what to expect when he had put in his official transfer request, but it had now become obvious that he was going to come in for a good deal of stick.

He issued his first words on the subject when he said, 'I am absolutely gutted at what is happening and now it is clear it is time for me to leave Everton. All clubs sell players, even Manchester United and Chelsea.'

And in response to the way that a faction of the fans had turned against him, he added, 'I am distressed at some of the things that have been said about me, especially considering that I know the truth.'

A couple of years later, chairman Kenwright put on a production in London called *A Few Good Men*. The same story had been made into a Hollywood film starring Jack Nicholson, Tom Cruise and Demi Moore, and the most memorable line was when Nicholson, in a military courtroom scene, bawled at his inquisitor (Cruise), 'You can't handle the truth!'

The truth of the matter in the Rooney transfer was actually quite simple. A young footballer with clear world-class potential wanted to move on to what he perceived was a bigger stage and, while he knew that he was going to find it tough, he felt that had no choice but to go ahead. He wanted to minimalise the distress to his family, tens of thousands of fans and the club that was ingrained on his heart.

But obviously it was going to upset people. It was one of those situations where it was impossible to keep everybody happy. The brutal reality was that he was going to a new employer. They were going to be paying his wages and, from then on, he owed them his loyalty.

For Everton's part, they didn't want him to go for obvious reasons, but when they knew that they had lost the battle to keep him, they then had to turn tough in the negotiations.

Surprisingly, given this sort of background, Kenwright – who has overseen hundreds of transfers to and from Goodison Park from all over the world – said that it was one of the most straightforward deals in which the club has ever been involved.

He commented, 'It wasn't a great problem. Once Wayne had made it clear he wanted to go, we got down to negotiations. They were pretty straightforward. There were no issues with the agent and we wrapped it up.'

There were, however, issues with a body of fans. Agent Paul Stretford's company, then called Proactive Sports Management, was bombarded with sick calls. Noisy protesters appeared outside the Rooney family home, while one unofficial Everton website posted details of Paul's home address, his car registration plate and his mobile phone number.

Rooney was at first saddened by the response from the fans and, in the months ahead, that sadness turned to anger as a faction of them continued to deride him. As far as he was concerned, it was a painful episode for a lot of people, but once the transfer was complete he thought that it was an issue that should be put to bed and that everybody should get on with their lives.

His inherent street toughness didn't always alert him to the sensitivities that people held over highly emotional issues, such as his transfer. For instance, it did not occur to him that posing next to the painted crest of his new club, just a few hours after his arrival at Old Trafford, would hurt so badly.

When Rooney is wounded, he slaps mud on it to stop it bleeding and gets on with his life; in contrast, many of us Toffees are still feeling a painful rawness.

But his first words as a United player were conciliatory. He said, 'It has been a tough week for everybody concerned with me. It is difficult because I have supported Everton all my life and, having played for them as well for the last two years, it made it even more difficult. I obviously made it clear that I wanted to leave Everton and once I knew that Manchester United were in for me, there was only one place that I was going to go.

'Over the last six weeks I made my mind up that I wanted to leave and Everton were aware of that ... There was a lot that happened behind the scenes, difficulties that people do not know about. But I want them to stay behind the scenes.

'It is tough on Evertonians, because they always saw

me as one of their own. Everton are a massive club and if they had been in the Champions League it would have been a different matter. But I had to move on for my career and there is no better place to do that than here at Manchester United.'

The boy wonder made it absolutely clear that it was a desire to play club football at a higher level that was his motivation to go – and further revealed that the experience of starring in Euro 2004 was the catalyst for his ambitions.

'After Euro 2004, I made up my mind that I wanted to play for a bigger club. The championships told me that I could play with top players in a big tournament and I wanted to start doing that week in week out ... When you are sitting there and a lot of the England players are talking about the Champions League, you want to be a part of that. It is the biggest club tournament in the world.'

This was the biggest factor in Rooney's decision to leave Everton. And it reveals much about his character.

All managers of teams full of internationals worry that when their players go away to join their national squads their heads could be turned by 'the grass is greener' effect. A youngster from a less fashionable club than Manchester United or Arsenal suddenly becomes more aware of the riches to be reaped by playing for a bigger club and this almost certainly happened to the then-eighteen-year-old Rooney as he suddenly started to feel at home in the company of the likes of David Beckham, Frank Lampard and Steven Gerrard.

He went to Portugal as an aspiring international player and Everton manager David Moyes probably didn't feel as though there was any great risk to the youngster having his ambitions fired by being in such exalted company. He may even have thought that the new kid on the block may well have been overawed by the whole event.

The world may not have known very much about Rooney then but, as the tournament progressed, it became clear that far from being overawed by the company in which he was playing, the Scouse firebrand was setting out his own agenda.

One of the hallmarks of his still-young career is a total absence of fear. All of his life he has played in teams where the other players have been three or four years older than himself. He doesn't yield to bigger men or bigger names and there hasn't been a stage built yet that would be too big for him.

One conversation with David Beckham about the night in Barcelona when Manchester United won the European Cup in such dramatic circumstances would have been enough to fire the ambition rockets that had been welded to his feet at birth.

It is clearly also in his nature to close one chapter simply to open another. After the conciliatory words on arriving at Old Trafford, he then decided to adopt the principle towards the Everton fans of, 'I will judge you as you judge me.'

He could not have cared less about a Liverpool fan throwing a mobile phone at him when he went to Anfield and scored the winner. He's never hidden his dislike of the Reds in his own city and has even admitted that he was dancing in the streets when Liverpool were 3-0 down in the Champions League final. But he clearly hasn't forgotten the angst that was generated in his city when he left.

In his first visit back to Goodison Park, fate had paired his past and present club together in the fifth round of the FA Cup. Tension built up in the days before the game: there were calls for increased security measures against protestors and even suggestions that Rooney may be stood down.

There was never the slightest hope of that happening. He made it clear that he was going to go into the lion's den with his head held high. He came out and warmed up at length before the kick-off and just ignored the abuse. United won.

At the start of Rooney's second season, Manchester United were due to play Everton in their opening game. This time he scored as United again won. His former team-mate Joseph Yobo sent a disastrous attempted back-pass almost to his feet and he gratefully accepted the gift.

Sometimes when footballers score against their old clubs, particularly on their home grounds, they shrug off the goal celebrations of their team-mates. Rooney celebrated in the way he celebrates any goal – arms waving, jumping and smiling.

More pointedly, when Manchester United equalised against Everton in the return fixture at Old Trafford later in the season, he took delight in the goal and made sure that the Everton fans knew it. He would say that he feels like that towards the fans of any team that he is playing against. Others would describe it as a merciless killer instinct.

In the weeks of speculation that ended with Rooney's transfer, there was another potential deal about to happen on Merseyside that also threatened to have an unpleasant fall-out. Immediately after the end of the Euro 2004 competition in Portugal, there was fervent speculation that Liverpool captain Steven Gerrard was on his way to Chelsea.

It had even been reported that the player had held talks with Chelsea just hours after England were knocked out of the competition. It became generally accepted among a faction of fans that, within a couple of weeks, he was going to the King's Road. There was a torrent of protest from Liverpool fans.

Gerrard had been frustrated by three seasons of under-achievement at Anfield and had been tormented for a year about his future. He hadn't had the greatest season and his performances in Euro 2004 fell way below his normally very high standards. But he had not anticipated the extent to which he had stirred up the anger of the fans. They didn't see three fallow seasons for a footballer in his prime as anything like a good enough excuse to move on to a club where he had a more likely chance of winning things. It all resulted in him receiving a bucketful of the same sort of bile that was now being dished out to Rooney.

It is believed that his family, in particular, came to the attention of the angry brigade and, for his own reasons, he decided to stay with Liverpool in the end. He can't regret his decision because, under new manager Rafael Benitez, he captained Liverpool as they won the European Cup in gripping style the following year.

Gerrard indicated that he stayed because the strength of protest about a potential move gave him a new perspective on the club that he had grown up with.

The legendary Diego Maradona keeps the Belgians busy during the World Cup in Spain, 1982

There are no villains in the Rooney transfer saga. In football, that's life. But there is one hero – and that's Wayne Rooney Sr.

He was placed in an impossible position. He lived the dream of every proud father who is a fanatical fan of a football club and who dreams that one day his son will wear the club shirt.

His boy was better than that. His lad was never going to struggle from an early age to break into football's professional ranks.

Before he was sixteen, the question 'How far can he go?' was being asked, and he was being compared to Maradona before he was eighteen.

The Bests of Belfast were the last family to be placed in such a situation, but they lived in the shadow of Ulster's shipbuilding yards and were never recognised as fanatical Manchester United supporters. Nor was George ever involved in a controversial transfer.

He established his court across the sea from Ireland and the family were never caught up in the vortex of uncontrollable madness that surrounded the man who was dubbed 'the fifth Beatle'.

The Rooneys did not have that buffer. They were at the churning centre of the maelstrom that was being whipped up by their boy's genius. For Wayne's dad, there was no hiding place. It may have been a stew that other fathers have faced before, but rarely have they had to do so in such a pressurised pot.

Perhaps the best comparable example is that of Rooney's England team-mate, Chelsea's midfield maestro Frank Lampard.

The Lampard family's unquestionable faith was West

Ham. Frank Sr had played for the club and became coach when Frank Lampard Jr was an up-and-coming player and an aspiring England international.

The club manager was Harry Redknapp, Frank Jr's uncle. The Lampards could not have been more recognisable as 'Hammers'.

When Harry and Frank Sr fell out with the chairman and left the club, Frank Jr felt disenfranchised and, after taking unfair criticism relating to nepotism, he moved to Chelsea.

His record since needs no justification, but he still receives tremendous stick whenever he goes back to Upton Park.

Frank Sr said, 'It saddens me. Some of it got really nasty, over the edge. Many of my best friends are West Ham fans and they are embarrassed about it.'

Wayne Rooney Sr – Everton fan and father of Manchester United superstar – knows how he feels.

THREE

ROONEY YOUTH

WAYNE ROONEY WAS born to be a footballer. He has never considered doing anything else.

'I'm going to play for Everton,' said Wayne Rooney, when, as an eight-year-old, he was asked by a teacher what he was going to do when he left school.

'But what will you do if that doesn't work out?' the teacher inquired. Being unusually positive for a boy of his years, he replied, 'It will work out. I am going to play for Everton.'

In normal circumstances, a teacher would have urged caution to such a huge ambition. Every little boy on Merseyside wanted to be a professional footballer – and the chances of even making it to apprentice ranks were about ten thousand to one.

'All I ever wanted to do was walk out at Goodison Park with our theme tune, *Z-Cars*, playing in the background. I wanted it so much ... As a kid, I used to get shivers down my spine when I heard it and I still do today.'

Wayne Rooney

But no teacher was going to argue with Wayne Rooney, even at his tender age. People know about football in and around Liverpool and anybody who had ever seen the youngster from Croxteth kick a ball, knew by instinct that this was no idle boast.

The first public recognition of the Rooney phenomenon came from train driver Bob Pendleton. Watching school-boys play soccer could be a thankless task, as Bob knew only too well. Talent scouting for his beloved club Everton was his sideline and an unquenchable passion, even on those bitterly cold winter's days when frost froze the ground.

Bob was a man who could spot raw talent a mile off. He'd watched hundreds of matches in his lifetime, most of them unmemorable, but every boy is a hero to his parents as he marches off the pitch to be consoled or congratulated.

It had been a long time, too long, since Bob had seen a lad with the kind of gift that could make the hairs on your head stand on end. He'd seen talent for sure, boys who could score good goals, who could dodge and weave, who could use their heads or who could make good passes. Brilliance, though, had passed them by and he was beginning to wonder if he'd ever experience the spine-tingling thrill of witnessing a new star in the making.

But every time he went to watch a match, he was wonderfully optimistic that he would discover 'his' star, a boy blessed with such stellar skill that he set the pitch ablaze.

Rooney was just nine years old, playing for Copplehouse Under-10s in the Walton and Kirkdale Junior Football League, but destiny was standing on the sidelines huddled in an anorak, and the boy's life was about to change forever.

Proud Bob, now sixty-four, recalls, 'You could tell he was special straightaway. When you see someone special, you just know, you feel your hair rising.'

It was a feeling only too familiar to the managers of the tiny Copplehouse Colts team, retired window cleaner Nev Davies and delivery driver John McKeown, both in their early forties.

They had taken a call from the pub team at the Western Approaches in 1994, who explained they were an Under-12 side, but that they had a boy playing for them who was just nine years old and who was a scoring sensation. Would they like to take a look? Would they! The duo shot over to the Rooney home in Croxteth the next evening.

Said McKeown, 'We headed over to the Rooney place and Wayne was outside, kicking a ball around in the street. We spoke to his mum and arranged to take a look at him the next day. Well, we had become quite blasé about meeting parents, giving trials and saying yes or no to young kids. This time we saw Wayne unleash a stunning overhead kick; he looked years ahead of anyone we had ever seen and we literally drove at 70mph back to his house to complete the signing. He was phenomenal. All he ever wanted to do was score and he was miles better than anyone else.'

And Nev, whose son Ryan used to set up young Rooney's goals from midfield, remembers predicting the fledgling star's rise to greatness.

He said, 'From the off, I said he would be better than Michael Owen or Robbie Fowler. He always had big, strong thighs and was more in the Alan Shearer mould, riding the tackles and playing with a fantastic awareness. Wayne was unbelievable ... always playing in the team a year above. We had him for eighteen months. Needless to say, he scored on his debut and once hit twelve in a fourteen-goal onslaught.

'In the first season he helped us to an Under-10s cup triumph and then we joined Liverpool's top league, the Walton and Kirkdale. He was fantastic there, too. He was so good he never practised with us. He was a throwback to when lads learned their craft in the street. But we picked him up in the mini-bus on Saturday morning, he'd listen to our instructions and off he would go.

'He was a shy lad, but very attentive. His dad, very often with his mum, was always there encouraging him. He never got on Wayne's back.

'After forty or so goals in the second season, John and I turned down the chance of a bet: that Wayne would become the youngest kid to play for Everton and then the youngest kid to play for England. Joe Royle pipped him to the Everton part, but after eclipsing Michael Owen as the Premiership's youngest scorer, the England bit – also held by Owen – was too good to miss!'

It was Nev who had tipped off scout Bob Pendleton

about the boy. Now, Bob stood rooted to the spot, transfixed by the sublime scene that was unfolding hypnotically before his eyes. It was a once-in-a-lifetime moment, a moment of unadulterated magic.

Said Bob, 'From the word go, the things Wayne could do with the ball, the goals he could score, you could tell he was a natural. Even then, he was so comfortable on the ball, he was just one of those born players ... amazing.'

Within minutes, buzzing with excitement, Bob hastily sought out team manager John McKeown.

He says, 'I approached their manager John and asked him, "What's the name of the little fellow?" He looked at me and groaned. "Oh Bobby," he said. "We've only just signed him. Leave him alone." I stared at him and said: "Leave him alone? You must be joking!"

'Wayne was strong, dedicated and couldn't stop scoring goals. The manager pointed out his mum and dad – big Wayne and Jeanette – over on the other side of the pitch. I went over and introduced myself and said that I'd like to take the young man into Bellefield for a trial at the Everton Academy. The look on their faces, because they were Evertonians, said it all. I knew I was on to a winner.'

The trouble was, arch-rivals Liverpool had got there first. The club's scouts had seen him performing in a Saturday league in the Bootle area and young Rooney had already been for a training session.

As Nev explains, 'A Liverpool scout had approached me and suggested Wayne have a trial. The Rooneys have always been true Blue, but they agreed I should take him along to Melwood because I was a Liverpool fan ... It was strange: he played well and scored several times in seven-a-side game, but the coaches were standoffish and didn't make a fuss of him.

'Wayne wasn't too disappointed. Next, I told Bob about him. He came to see him and his eyes immediately lit up. This time John, because he supports Everton, went with Wayne and his mum to the Everton Academy, where his performance was noted straightaway. It was the end of the 1995–96 season and Wayne never played for Copplehouse again.'

Bob takes up the story, recalling in the *Guardian*: 'On the Thursday, I went over and had a little chat with Ray Hall, the director of Everton's Academy and said, "I'm bringing the little fellow in."

'Wayne had been for a training session with Liverpool, but he only ever wanted to do one thing and that was to play for Everton. It wouldn't have mattered what Liverpool said to him, he wouldn't have gone there. His dad, Wayne Sr, also said he wasn't going anywhere else. He was also adamant that he wasn't going to end up with Liverpool.

'Wayne has set the city on fire. He was born to score goals. It's a real *Roy of the Rovers* story.

'I've been asked if I think I'll ever find another Rooney and the answer is always the same – "Jesus, no!" A good friend said to me, "You only find one of them in your lifetime, so sit back and enjoy the ride Wayne is going to give you," – and I am enjoying it. It's emotional at times, but I'm sure Wayne's going through the same!'

Lifelong Everton fan Rob 'Macca' McCarthy, thirty-one, also remembers the first time he saw young Rooney and began to see for himself that the rumours about a new wonder kid could actually be true.

'I went down to Croxteth one Sunday to watch him playing for a pub team. It was the Western Approaches (The Wezzy) and other players in the team were all in their mid-twenties and looked the sort that loved a good punch-up. Most of them had flattened noses and close-cropped hair. The opposition team were from Speke in south Liverpool and they, too, looked just like the 'broken-nose brigade'.

'When I first set eyes on Wayne, I thought he was going to get eaten alive by the opposition players, who would not have looked out of place as club doormen. But my fears were unfounded and I couldn't believe what I was seeing as Wayne left his prey for dead. As he raced forward with the ball, several of the opposing players would try to kick lumps out of him, but he danced and weaved his way though them.

'I honestly thought that he was going to get hurt by these men, but he gave as good as he got: I heard a couple of the opposing players squeal and groan as they went down under one of Wayne's bone-crunching tackles.

'This was a schoolboy playing, and holding his own, against grown men who liked nothing better than intimidating and giving their opponents harsh tackles. Well, it was they who received a lesson, because nothing that they could do had any effect on young Wayne. He was not in the slightest bit afraid of them. He was fearless.

'Wayne went on to score two goals and had a hand in the third with his team winning 3-1.

'I still wonder to this day if the opposing players knew that he was only a schoolboy, as they would kick him up in the air and watch as he got back up to come back for more.

'I went to watch him on a number of occasions after that. He had the aggression of Graeme Souness and the skills of Diego Maradona and Kenny Dalglish all rolled into one.

'The touchline would be jam-packed with people who had come just to see Wayne play; even arthritic pensioners who would sit there in wheelchairs with their check blankets over their laps. It was probably the only time they would bother to venture outdoors in the week – and this was in the dead of winter.

'That's the effect that Wayne had on people. These same pensioners were comparing him to the great Duncan Edwards, one of the Busby Babes who perished in the Munich air disaster in 1958: these comparisons were being made by old men who had actually seen Duncan Edwards play. They would also compare him to Billy Liddle, a Liverpool footballing legend from many years ago and they were making these comparisons about a lad who was still in school. He was simply phenomenal.'

Everton's Academy director Ray Hall has worked on the club's youth development scheme for twelve years and has coaxed and cajoled a galaxy of future stars through their paces. But even he was gripped by an instantaneous thrill when he first witnessed Rooney in action. He signed the boy after just one training session.

'I didn't even need that as proof. When you get an experienced scout sitting there quivering while you're talking to the lad, you know he's a special talent,' he told the *Guardian*.

'We had started hearing a lot about this lad, even when he was an Under-9 player. When Bob brought him in, he was trembling and he was spilling his tea all over the place because he was so excited.'

Ray knew he had a rare talent on his hands, but it wasn't until he took the lad with an Under-11 team to play at Manchester United's training ground that he recognised that his latest signing was sprinkled with magic.

Wayne was just ten years old, but he delivered a performance so stunning that it hushed the awed crowd into silence.

Ray recalls, 'It was an eight-a-side match on small pitches with small goals. There were hundreds of people there. All the parents were on one side of the pitch and the coaches were on the other as the match started. Someone played a ball over. The ball was crossed, but it went behind Wayne. Instead of controlling it or trying to head it, he executed a scissor-kick from 10 to 15 yards out and the ball flew straight into the top corner of the net. There was total silence around the ground; you could have heard a pin drop. Out of nowhere, I heard one parent – Wayne's dad I think – start to clap. Then it became a slow ripple of applause and within a few seconds everyone was clapping him like thunder, even the United parents were applauding. It was unforgettable.'

The boy wonder later went on to score a record-breaking ninety-nine goals for the Academy's Under-10s in one season.

Hall's department is one of the biggest at Everton, because producing their own homegrown talent is crucial for the cash-strapped club.

He says, 'There is something about this area, because it has always produced outstanding talent, not only for us but also for Liverpool and Tranmere Rovers. It must be in the genes. Francis Jeffers came here aged nine and was in the first team as a teenager. Wayne was the same age when he arrived. They are both local lads, they went to the same junior and secondary schools and they both made their full England debuts together against Australia.

'You can never be sure how far a young boy will progress in football, but Franny and Wayne were always at the top of their age groups in both ability and potential.

'I remember the first time I saw Franny and it was obvious that he was an intelligent and gifted lad. He scores most of his goals inside the penalty area, but that is a knack in itself. With Wayne, the goals can come from anywhere, because he is physically the stronger of the pair.

'In recent years, we have produced four England internationals in Jeffers, Rooney, Michael Ball and Gavin McCann, plus Richard Dunne for the Republic of Ireland. And five of the ten youngest goalscorers in the Premiership came from here – Jeffers and Rooney again, plus Ball, Michael Branch and Danny Cadamarteri.

'Since our Academy was established in 1995, seventeen players have gone on to play for the first team.

'Wayne has done brilliantly. Every challenge he has been faced with he has met and raised the bar. Nothing seems to faze him. He has always played over his own age, which is probably why he's so comfortable with the England squad. He's the youngest, but he's used to that. He's no different from the kid at school who is a gifted mathematician and who has been moved up classes to be with kids of his own ability.'

The Everton Academy was truly a family affair for the Rooneys – back in 1998, Wayne and his brothers Graham and John all played for the club's youth teams. John remains, but Graham has left to concentrate on the family's second love, boxing.

Says Ray, 'It was the first time in history that we had three brothers all playing here at the same time, and all of them were talented.'

As with all kids at the Academy, Wayne was taken under the wing of a welfare officer from the moment he was signed up. It's the officer's job to keep an eagle eye on the boys' development, to ensure that they are not

Boxing is almost as important to Rooney's family as football, and his younger brother Graham is a keen amateur fighter.

under too much pressure and to prevent them from becoming unhealthily obsessed by performance.

Gently, over time, the youngsters are schooled in the pitfalls of fame: how to behave in a fashion that brings credit to the game and how to handle attention from the public and media.

Ray says, 'There are five bubbles surrounding a player. Every player has to cope with his own rate of technical development, physical growth, physiological progress and mental development. We have technical coaches and fitness coaches and a medical department and sports scientists, but by far the biggest bubble is their social and emotional development.

'At Goodison Park, players are presented with a code of conduct and every year they are reminded that they have a duty to behave well. If we've done anything for Wayne, we've improved his social life and skills. He was a timid boy when he came here, but we give the players life-skills training on how to manage the media and everything else that goes with the glitz.'

It wasn't just Wayne's scintillating skill that stood out, but also his mental strength: he was a shy, taciturn boy who kept his thoughts to himself. However, he was already developing the focused discipline that would catapult him on to the world stage with lightning speed.

> Wayne was such a talented player he joined Everton's Youth Academy while still at De La Salle secondary school. He then went straight into the first team squad.

The practice pitches used by the Academy were a mile away from De La Salle, the Catholic school where Rooney was a pupil. Yet he was always the first to arrive, leaping on his BMX bike the second the school bell rang at 3.30pm and pedalling as fast as his legs could carry him to the patchily turfed theatre of his dreams.

There, alone, he re-created his favourite goals: zig-zagging across the pitch and shooting over and over again with a vivid commentary running in his head, until training started at 5pm.

Said Hall, 'Wayne never missed a session, never gave us a moment's problem and had this terrific, supportive family that let us get on with the job.'

His former PE teacher at De La Salle, Joe Hennighan, also remembers Rooney's dedication: 'Wayne was not particularly academic – young lads love sport and if you live in this city there is only one sport they are going to play, and that is football. Once Wayne started playing, it was obvious that he was going to go far. He was a really good competitor and was always very able physically.'

The school, based in tough, inner-city Croxteth, has built a reputation as a breeding ground for top-class footballers – Francis Jeffers was also a pupil and Wayne would later go on to partner him in the duo's first appearances in England's full squad in the friendly against Australia: a hearty consolation for De La Salle after losing its best players to the Everton Academy.

Teachers at De La Salle comprehensive still speak of how they would jostle at a first-floor window in awe to get a glimpse of the giant of a lad in the 20-a-side kickabouts taking place below on their playground.

Rooney, always a stocky lad, suddenly shot up in size when he was thirteen; he towered over the other boys in his class.

Said Joe, 'Wayne was the biggest lad in his class and his size was the thing you always noticed first. I've always said you've got to be strong to get a muffin in the dinner queue at De La Salle!'

Briefly, Wayne's football form suffered as his body adapted and he struggled to master his limbs, but his unerring discipline never wavered. His worried parents would often call the Academy, concerned that their son had not returned home, but Wayne, more often than not, would be found pounding the treadmill at the specially equipped gym.

MARQUIS OF QUEENS-BURY

Sometimes, though, as with any boy, Wayne's halo slipped. He would naughtily sneak off to the local bookies with a pal to play on the fruit machines – his height made him appear older than his years – or he would stride off to his Uncle Richie's boxing gym for a bout of body-building and sparring with his cousin in Croxteth.

His fuming mum, Jeanette, would tear him off a strip when the lad eventually rode up at home, attempting to look a picture of innocence, but despondently knowing that his mum – as is the case with all mums – had eyes in the back of her head and beyond.

Today, at 5ft 10in, Wayne's an average height for a player, but his bulk – he's 12st 4lb – and his wide-shouldered boxer's physique, make him an unstoppable bulldozer on the pitch. That and Wayne's cleanness of shot have invited comparisons with former England skipper Alan Shearer. And that's music to the ears of Rooney.

As a youngster, he avidly studied his hero until details of the superstar's legendary goal-getting were etched into his memory. He would later take to the street for an action replay, placing himself in the shoes of Shearer.

'He'd be my ideal strike partner,' Wayne told the official Everton website, 'because I used to watch him as a kid and I tried to model myself around him.'

Wayne's star was soon fixed in the firmament at the Everton Academy. He blazed through like a comet. At Under-12 level, he played for the Under-13s; at Under-15 he played for the Under-17s and even the Under-19s. By sixteen, he was playing with the professionals.

One man remembers the fourteen-year-old Rooney only too well. Walter Smith, then Everton manager, was sitting in his office at the training ground, tackling paperwork, when he chanced to look up. Outside on the pitch, an Under-17 game was in full flow. Suddenly, Smith felt as though he had been struck by a bolt of lighting, as a bulky, shaven-haired lad let rip a bullet-like shot from the halfway line.

He said, 'I just took a couple of minutes to have a look at the game going on outside. I saw this kid run a yard into the opposition half and then unleash this magnificent shot. I don't think it went in, but I remember thinking to myself, "My God, who *is* that?"

Alan Shearer, the Premiership's greatest ever goalscorer, believes that Wayne Rooney is a match for any Brazilian player – even Ronaldinho, the man who has twice been voted World Player of The Year.

He said, 'Wayne Rooney is England's Ronaldinho. They are different players, but Wayne is every bit as talented. I'm not sure that anybody has ever been as good for England as Wayne Rooney. I'm not sure that anybody ever  **will be. He's sensational – even at his early age. He can only get better with every big tournament. Wayne hates getting beaten at anything, which is a very good thing. And with Michael Owen he forms a great international partnership.'**

'It was something I had only ever seen Pelé and David Beckham try. Not many would try that, never mind a youngster. When I asked who he was, our youth team coach Colin Harvey told me and then said: "By the way boss, he's only fourteen!" I was amazed.'

Smith, talking in the *People*, added, 'When Wayne was only fourteen, Colin would use him as a sub for the Under-17s and when he was fifteen he was playing in the Under-18 and Under-19 teams. And he would come on and score nearly every time. We realised we had a youngster who was very special ... Going into the training ground on a Saturday morning before first team games at Goodison, I'd watch Wayne playing against much older boys, scoring goals from every angle. It was incredible.'

Once Rooney had tackled the problems posed by his teenage hormones, he was ready to start tackling on the pitch again – and scoring the kind of spectacular goals usually confined to the peak of the Premiership.

To his joy, the devoted Toffeeman got his chance to stuff Liverpool in the first Under-19 Merseyside derby of the 2001 season.

Hundreds of fans had converged on Everton's training ground, Bellefield, and those in the red shirts of Liverpool were smugly anticipating victory with their team sitting on a 2-1 lead with just fifteen minutes to go until the final whistle.

Rooney watched anxiously from the bench, every fibre of his body tense, fervently hoping that he'd get the chance to help his team grab victory from the drooling Red jaws of defeat. Then, as Liverpool got ready to take a corner, Everton brought on their deadliest weapon from their schoolboy arsenal.

Walter Smith, who as Everton manager during Rooney's time at the youth academy was astonished by Wayne's precocious talent.

Rooney strolled onto the pitch; a few moments later, Everton equalised. Then, with just nail-biting minutes to spare, Rooney struck a supernova volley from the edge of the penalty area that exploded into the Liverpool net. It was the last kick of the game and it instantly wiped out the smiles on the Reds' faces: result − 3-2 to Everton; result − 'Roomania' was born. And he was still only sixteen.

The dismay of the Liverpool fans hung heavy in the air and, later that week, the club made a raid for Rooney, hoping to prise him away from Goodison Park. But the boy stayed resolutely stuck and pledged his future to the Everton Academy. Such was the club's relieved glee, it triumphantly paraded Rooney in front of 38,615 fans during the half-time interval of a Premiership game against Derby County on 15 December.

One reason that Wayne would never have gone anywhere was because of the effect of youth team coach Colin Harvey, who had built up a strong relationship with the youngster over a number of years.

Harvey, himself a legend among Evertonians as a championship winner in 1970 and as someone who had managed the club, has admitted he literally rubbed his eyes the first time he saw Rooney. In his bestselling diary of memoirs, *Everton Secrets*, he wrote:

'He's undoubtedly the best young player I've ever seen, the best Everton have produced and he can become one of the greatest English players of all time. Until Wayne came along, the best youngster I'd ever seen was Alan Ball. I later teamed up with Bally at Goodison and he did it all for Everton and England, winning seventy-two caps, the World Cup and championship medals. He was the best Everton player in my opinion and my experience.

'My earliest memory comes from a Sunday morning in August 1997 when there was a break in the Under-16s game because of an injury. I happened to glance over to where the Under-11s were playing. As I looked, this kid got the ball on the halfway line, went past four opponents and lashed it into the net. That was my first sight of him – he was still a couple of months away from his twelfth birthday. So I left the Under-16s match and went to see more of this lad in the Under-11 team.

'Any thoughts that what I'd seen was merely a freak were soon dispelled. Wayne did remarkable things on a regular basis. He was stronger than the rest of the kids and I did wonder whether he would develop or level out when the others caught up with him physically. I've seen it happen so often. But not with Wayne. He developed and maintained his strength. I just looked at him and thought that if he carried on like that, he was going to be a world-beater.'

Harvey was also anxious to try and direct Wayne off the pitch as well as on it. He said, 'I used to give him a lift to his home in Croxteth, or to his grandmothers, after we had got back from games. I'd have a little word in his ear and give him bits of advice about whom he was knocking around with. I told him he must continue to work hard at school. Wayne was always very receptive to things like that. He'd listen and take it all on board. He wasn't an introvert, but very much a quiet, self-contained lad. That was until he stepped onto the field, which is, and always has been, his playground. He always knew exactly how good he was.

Colin Harvey, Everton youth team coach and staunch early supporter of Rooney's blossoming talent.

Even as a youngster I'd pay to watch him play and I mean it.

'Wayne has very kindly said in public that I have helped to make him a better player. But I agree with what Bill Shankly once said, that it's not coaches that make players but mothers and fathers and he's got great parents. All coaching can do is bring out skills and help their natural expression, but all that is meaningless unless you have the sort of inborn talent that the boy possesses. Even if Wayne was having a bad game, he would still do three or four things in a match that would take your breath away. He'd do something that would make your heart beat a little bit faster.'

Wayne's career was moving at lightning pace and he would soon be on the verge of the first team. But before moving forever into a new stratosphere, Rooney had a single aim: to lift the Football Association Youth Cup with Everton.

The mesmeric striker was rarely halted on his successful mission, ramming home thunderbolt goals in almost every match. Against Manchester City he scored twice in a 4-2 victory. West Bromwich Albion fared no better, falling victim to the dazzling skills of their young opponent as he bobbed and weaved his way past players as if they were mere shadows and rocketed home two riveting goals, lobbing the keeper from 20 yards for his crushing finale.

> Wayne's former home in Croxteth now lies empty. But scratched on one of the windows is the legend 'WR, Rooney E.F.C.' – the graffiti of a footballing dreamer, but one whose dreams were on the verge of coming true.

Nottingham Forest met the same fate in the quarter-finals, with Rooney executing an amazing scissor-kick for the first goal against their Youth Cup rivals. Later, he set up a goal for defender David Carney, who thumped home the winner in the 2-1 triumph.

But it was the match against Tottenham Hotspur at White Hart Lane that would start the wave of fruitless bids for Rooney's talent. Spurs manager Glenn Hoddle was gob smacked by the boy's soul-tingling performance – and was dispirited to discover that he wasn't for sale. The reason was obvious: Rooney had already created a 3-1 lead on aggregate for the Everton team when, in the thirty-seventh minute, he unleashed a goal so spectacular that all anybody could do was gawp in wonder, including Hoddle.

> **Wayne was a central part of the Everton Youth Team that reached the final of the FA Youth Cup in 2002. He scored 8 goals in as many games during the same cup run, including the famous amazing 30-yard strike against Tottenham.**

Everton had been given a free-kick 30 yards from goal and Rooney, never one to miss an opportunity, reckoned he might just fly one into the net. He sent a disappointing shot curling straight into the Spurs wall but, as the ball cascaded down out of the air, Rooney appeared like magic to take it on his chest and, before it had a chance to kiss the earth, sent it crashing into the top corner with his left foot.

The Roon of the Rovers story didn't end there – he went on to score eight during the campaign, one short of the record shared by Liverpool's Michael Owen and Arsenal's Jeremie Aliadiere, and had twenty-five goal notches on his goalpost by the end of the season.

The best, however, was yet to come.

FOUR

LOVE ME ROO

UNLIKE MOST FOOTBALLERS' relationships, Rooney's romance with fiancée Coleen began way back when he was a schoolboy and those solid foundations are what have sustained the couple through stormy times.

Wayne has been accused of cheating on Coleen and it was rumoured that the incensed Coleen even threw her £25,000 engagement ring into a squirrel sanctuary near their former Formby home. But the trials and tribulations of fame, resulting in the dirty linen being washed in public with the heartbreaking allegations that go with it, have only served to forge a deeper respect and love between the young couple.

Said Coleen, 'He is the person I love and who I want to stay with for the rest of my life. Friends and family had warned me against dating him. They also tried to persuade me that we were too young to set up home. But I have no regrets, because I will stand by him no matter what. I had no hesitation when Wayne proposed to me and we've been engaged for two years now.

'People think that we are too young, but I don't believe that. If you are in love and want to spend your life with someone it doesn't matter what age you are. My mum was married at eighteen and recently celebrated her twenty-fifth wedding anniversary.'

The couple's romance has survived, despite claims that Wayne had visited a Liverpool brothel – allegations he initially hotly denied, insisting that he had been the victim of a sting.

Wayne's tattoo of a celtic cross with his fiancée's name above.

Further claims surfaced when pretty brunette Emily Fountain, twenty, claimed that the footballer took her to a private room in a nightclub and kissed her. The computer sales girl said she snogged Rooney at the trendy Odyssey Bar in Altrincham, Cheshire, as he celebrated victory over Chelsea with a group of his team-mates.

But Coleen told the *Daily Mirror*: 'There are some evil and jealous people out there who clearly want to spoil things between Wayne and I, but there are more important things to think about and they should give it a rest. Nothing will come between us. We'd barely been together a year when he got my name tattooed on his arm.

'Now we're still happily together after three years and I think it's a lovely lasting gesture. I'm so in love. Wayne even calls me before every match and from the moment I wake up in the morning I think about him all day. Wayne is happy that I am happy and vice versa. We're engaged, so we're going to get married some day, but we haven't set a date; we haven't even thought that far ahead. We love each other and that means we will be with each other as long as we are alive.'

It was Wayne who romanced Coleen, not the other way round – and she made him work at it all the way ... she still does. If anything, he is more in love with her and more in need of her genuine frankness and friendship than ever before.

Said Wayne, 'I want Coleen to be happy – that makes me happy. It worries me that she might feel lonely when I'm training or whatever, so I'm always encouraging her to go out shopping or to go and see her mates. I want her to enjoy her life. What I'm doing, it's for us, not just me.

We're a team, that's the way it is and I want for her to be happy. She's the most special person in my life. She's not just beautiful on the outside, she's beautiful on the inside, too.

'She's gorgeous looking, but she's also got a great personality. She's a dead special person and I can't think of anybody who's a patch on her. From the

moment I kissed her – I was just fourteen – I always knew she was the girl for me and that feeling never changed. It just stayed strong and I enjoy every moment with her.

The superstar revealed that the trappings of talent, fame and money don't make much impact upon their life together: 'We're just ordinary, normal people. We have a glass of wine and watch TV, usually *EastEnders* or *Coronation Street*, and then go to bed, where I'll watch a DVD and Coleen falls asleep. She thinks 10pm is late, but then she has to get me up for training with a cuppa, because I hate getting out of bed.'

Coleen continued, 'We are each other's best friend. Wayne is away a lot playing football, but I think it is healthy to have space in a relationship and I make sure that I am never on my own. It makes it more special when we are together. When Wayne has been away, it's exciting and we can't wait to see each other. If we were together constantly, it wouldn't be so special. We love doing simple things, like snuggling up on the sofa and watching *X Factor*. It's Wayne's favourite, we both think it's dead good.

'And we still like going down the chippie sometimes to get our dinner. I have to admit, I love Italian food now: I am a big fan of pasta and it is nice going out to fancy restaurants. But nothing beats my mum's roast dinners. We always go round to my mum's for Sunday roast.

'We're just normal people. I wash our clothes while Wayne has a lie in or I do the tidying up while he plays on the computer. We're not big breakfast eaters, but I love making him tea and toast to have in bed.

'I write my magazine column on a Sunday, so Wayne

watches Spanish football ... or some foreign team; he loves it, it's his job.

'Everyone says what a leap our change of lifestyle has been, but I don't see it that way. There is a difference in the attention I get, but I am still the same person underneath. I'd say the biggest change is that I have done so many more things and travelled a lot, which has been amazing.

'When I was young, we would go on family holidays, but not to the extent of being able to have a weekend in Madrid and a fantastic two-week holiday in Barbados. I think that's one of the highlights now.'

'I'm so proud of Wayne,' she went on reveal in an interview with *Hello!* magazine. 'When he picked up the FIFA Young Player of the Year award it was just brilliant ... Sometimes, when I see him out on the pitch at Old Trafford with all those thousands of people screaming, I think, "My God, look at all these people coming here to watch Wayne and the team."

'I often say to him: "What does it feel like to be out there?" Now and again he will stop and take it all in and he will say: "Did you hear them all shouting nice things?" and he will come home on a high.

'The fans play such a big part, that's what he always says; they are the ones who come and pay to see the team play and Wayne respects that, particularly the ones who travel away, he always says how great they are.

'The thing is, I'm still not big on football. Wayne has tried to teach me about the offside rule, but I still don't understand it ... I like football, but I only really enjoy watching when Wayne is playing ... but he also knows

On holiday in Barbados.

that I am his biggest fan. He is definitely "The One".'

Wayne is renowned for his tight-lipped silence and monosyllabic answers in public, but he says, 'People think I'm this shy boy, but when you get to know me I can be dead loud. I do take a while to come out of my shell; I don't jump in feet first when I meet people, I'm quite cautious. But I like having a laugh and I don't mind sending myself up once I've got to know people.

'I'm a lad whose Michael Jackson impression can clear the dance floor – and I can sing like Will Young. I've always loved singing. I'm always saying to Coleen that if I hadn't been a footballer, I would have got on *X Factor*. Coleen can laugh – and she does. But I know it's only because I am such a fantastic singer ... I'll often sing to her in the morning, usually something by Usher ... it's the music I psyche myself up with before a match. Or I'll belt out Robbie Williams' "Let Me Entertain You" or something by Will Young.

'When I was a kid I had a karaoke machine in my bedroom and I'd stand there in front of the mirror, singing a slushy Westlife number or something by the Stereophonics. I also love 50 Cent, Eminem ... and Lionel Richie is another favourite. I don't quite get the high pitch, but I still like to practise – as a kid, I even stood there singing with a hairbrush when there was no microphone to hand.

'I also enjoy a good dance. In fact, I bought a Michael Jackson DVD so I could practise my moves at home

Rooney favourite Robbie Williams was forced to cancel a party performance for Rooney's eighteenth birthday and engagement to fiancée Coleen McLoughlin due to scheduling problems.

before we went to Euro 2004 – and my moonwalk is brilliant!

'My circumstances have changed, but I'm still the same person inside; I'm still the kid who sang into his hairbrush and kicked a ball around in the street. I am still me and I still like doing the same things and still have the same feelings. Sometimes, people act as if I have won the lottery or something, as if everything just happened for me overnight, but that's not the way it was.

'I used to go training five nights a week and then play a match every Saturday or Sunday. While my mates were off down to the cinema, I'd be putting my kit on to train. There were times when I didn't want to go, when I just wanted to give it all up. I wanted to hang out with my mates, go to the cinema and just do normal stuff. But my mum and dad would say to me: "If you want to be a professional footballer, you have to make sacrifices," and they would put me in the car and drive me to the training ground.

'I was only a kid and I felt as though I was missing out on life because I couldn't be with the other lads and couldn't do the things they were doing. I loved my football, but at a young age what you want to do most is to be one of the gang, to hang out with your mates and just kick a ball in the street. I had to be disciplined and committed to get where I am now and I've worked hard for it.

'I don't see myself as any kind of hero. People pay you all these compliments and it's an honour, but you could start to believe it all if you're not careful; Coleen skits me about it – if I've got a bit of a cob on she'll say: "Who do you think you are, Pelé?"

Coleen is known as an avid shopper, but this time she has an excuse – filming a commercial in Knightsbridge, London!

'It's Coleen who really knows me better than anyone else. Our relationship has come a long, long way and there's nothing we don't share.'

One of Coleen's bugbears is the way she is presented in the media. She says, 'I am made out to be somebody totally different to the person my friends and family know and it does upset me. I don't think I have ever been in a position to take my feet off the ground because of my strong family background and because I have all of my friends around me. It's impossible for me not to be me anymore. It just wouldn't happen.

'I get criticised for the things I wear or for the way I look, but I'm not going to dress up for the paparazzi every day. People shouldn't be judged on what they wear. Some days I will be lush because I have put on a nice top and jeans to go and see my mum and then the next day I can be dressed in an old tracksuit and looking terrible, usually all sweaty from the gym. You can't worry about it.

'The only person whose judgement I care about is Wayne. He never gives me advice on clothes. He hates clothes shopping, but he is always appreciative of the way I look. If he does pick something, I tend to go for the opposite. If I like something I wear it, but I am quite conservative in the way I dress. Wayne and my dad would kill me if I wore something too revealing.'

The couple's fledgling romance started at school, where the passion that burned in Rooney's soul and set his feet alight had already made him a playground hero, idolised by classmates who would line up to take turns in the break-time kick-abouts organised by their star player.

Soccer was his obsession and it occupied his every waking moment but, like any teenage lad, he had another burgeoning interest: girls.

Already standing head and shoulders above his classmates, well-built and with a reputation as a boy's own hero, Wayne cut an impressive figure on the tough Croxteth council estate that he called home. But he was a bashful lad, quiet and shy. The company of males was his comfort zone, either in the rough and tumble of his uncle's boxing gym, among the light-hearted banter of the soccer changing room or on the testosterone-charged terraces at Goodison Park.

The acne-plagued awkwardness of youth, with limbs and hair sprouting, hormones running wild and emotions sky-high, hadn't passed him by. But Wayne couldn't afford to be distracted and, anyway, the cocky charm of the skirt-chaser wasn't in his nature. He was already too streetwise, too thoughtful, too self-aware for that, and what's more, he had been counselled by parents who were only too familiar with the pitfalls of estate living.

Single motherhood was a fact of life on many of the estate's streets and within his own extended family; his dad's favourite pub, The Dog and Gun, on the corner of the road where they lived, had closed down after a police investigation into drug dealing; and petty vandalism was rife.

The potential for brief, but potent, youthful fumblings that shatter dreams had also been carefully explained to Wayne at the Everton Academy, where a glittering future now lay within his grasp. Avoid temptation and confine conquest to the pitch: a wised-up Wayne understood the value of cautious discipline.

Still, there were girls, those he knew as friends: the sisters of his pals; his cousins; his classmates ... but one girl in particular had captivated the wary lad and his affected boyish indifference slowly evaporated as he came to recognise the unsettling feelings she evoked in him.

Although he didn't know it at the time, Rooney was falling in love. And Coleen McLoughlin, the local beauty he now plans to wed, was the girl who had captured his heart.

Says Coleen, 'We're as much in love as we were back then. Our lifestyle isn't much different. Wayne eats more salad – chicken Caesar is his favourite – and I'm big on pasta. I eat porridge for breakfast, nothing fancy, but crisps are still my downfall.

'We don't go out much midweek, although sometimes we'll pop into our favourite restaurant, Wing's in Manchester, for a Chinese – my favourite is chicken in black bean sauce and Singapore vermicelli.

'I take a multivitamin, primrose oil and iron tablet every day, which I never did until I started training in the gym; that's one change, but hardly a big one. And my best beauty tip is Vaseline – you can't beat it for dry lips and skin – and Touche Eclat for dark circles if you've had a bit of a session the night before,' she told *You* magazine.

Coleen, a pony-tailed, dark-blonde girl with clear, green eyes, was just twelve years old when she first met Rooney. She was a pupil at the strict, all-girls St John Bosco Roman Catholic school where Wayne's mum, Jeanette, worked as a part-time cleaner, and was a friend of Claire, the sister of one of the soccer star's favourite cousins, Thomas.

It was Thomas's dad Richie who owned the boxing gym where Wayne and his younger brothers Graham and John would often sit and watch football matches on the widescreen telly with their mates, including Coleen's brothers Anthony and Joe.

Eight families from the close-knit Rooney clan were neighbours on the Croxteth estate and the tentacles of their friendships often crossed.

Says Coleen, 'I can remember Wayne playing football in the street with my brothers. We were only twelve when we first met and we were all just mates at first.'

Coleen's parents Colette, forty-two, a hospice care worker, and Antony, forty-five, a labourer, lived a few minutes' walk around the corner from Wayne's family and, like Wayne Sr, her dad had been a keen amateur boxer.

He helped Wayne's uncle, Richie, to run the boxing gym and had coached young Rooney there as a boy. The families shared an earnest Roman Catholic faith and a fierce desire to see their children succeed.

> **Wayne's surname is found mainly in Ireland. It dates back to the thirteenth century. A genealogy website states that Rooney is the anglicised version of 'O'Ruanaidh', from 'Ruanadh', a personal name meaning 'champion'. The principle family with that name originated in County Down.**

Wayne was comfortable around Coleen. She was a no-nonsense girl who, like him, harboured driving ambition. Since the age of six, she had wanted to be an actress and, like him, was hard-working and wholly dedicated to her goal.

Said Wayne, 'I had to walk past Coleen's house every day to get to school. Our families knew each other because Coleen's dad helped run the gym where my dad boxed. At that stage, I didn't really know Coleen and I just used to hang around with other lads up the road.

'Still, by the time I was fourteen I knew I fancied her. But Coleen wasn't really interested in boys. She was a goody who did her homework. All I was interested in was football.'

With a maturity beyond their years, they both recognised that their ambitions would necessitate sacrifice, a fact that became glaringly obvious when Wayne's starburst talent catapulted him into the spotlight on a world stage.

While he dazzled on the pitch in England's 2-0 win over Turkey in England's Euro 2004 qualifiers, Coleen remained at home to star as Fat Sam in her school's production of *Bugsy Malone* and, earlier, she had stayed behind to sit an English exam while he flew out to join the England squad at Spain's La Manga camp for preseason training.

Even today, as the future wife of England's brightest star, her ambition remains. She says, 'I've always known I wanted to act and I want to be recognised for what I achieve, not only for being with Wayne. I enjoy being with him, don't get me wrong – he's dead caring and he makes me feel special. He cheers me up with his funny sense of humour, he's a great mimic and he's always doing impressions of people off the telly.

'I still find it hard to believe that my Wayne is the Wayne Rooney who gets his name chanted on the pitch.

When he scores, I have to look back and think, "That's my Wayne, the man I love." I can hardly believe it, it doesn't seem real.

'Afterwards, when I'm on my own, I read about the goals in the newspapers and I get a huge surge of love and pride.'

The green shoots of the couple's romance grew from a steady, innocent friendship, one that flourished on the street corners of Croxteth, before love began to bud.

As the afternoon light began to fade, Wayne would often ride out on his mountain bike to fetch paper-wrapped chips from his local chippie, returning to find Coleen sitting on a wall, watching as her brothers and their mates played footie. He'd plonk himself down beside her, offering her chips with a nonchalance that belied his beating heart.

Said Coleen, 'We used to spend hours hanging around on the street corner, just talking to each other. At first we were just mates, but then we began to spend more time together and we became best friends – Wayne knows me better than anyone else.'

But Wayne was too shy to ask Coleen for a formal date. She was the girl next door he'd known since childhood: an ambitious, bright girl who he counted as a trusted friend. He was uncertain whether the tender affection he felt towards her was returned and, in a quandary, played the joker to try and gauge her feelings.

The star admitted, 'I used to pull little stunts to try and get close to her because until I know people I can be quite shy ... I desperately wanted to kiss her, but I didn't know how. I remember once I pretended to have contact lenses that I couldn't get in my eyes and asked her to have a look and see if my eyes were okay.

'I could never get the courage to ask her out properly or kiss her. I used to try and ask, but she wouldn't take it seriously. I invited her out on loads of dates – to the chippie, to the pictures, I even promised to take her to Paris for Valentine's Day if she'd come on a date. She was gorgeous looking and had a great personality, but she always thought I was skitting her.'

It wasn't until Wayne turned knight in shining armour, riding to the rescue after spotting his princess in trouble, that he managed to win his date – and then, only after enlisting the help of Claire, his cousin and Coleen's friend.

He said, 'My day came when the chain came off Coleen's bike. She was with my cousin Claire and I saw them trying to fix it. I was on my way home and stopped to help. I used it as an excuse to chat to Coleen, asking if I could borrow her video of *Grease*. I've always been a fan. I loved that movie and knew she did too.

'When Coleen went inside to get the video, I grabbed Claire and asked her to get Coleen to come on a date with me. By then, I was fed up of asking. But this time, Coleen said yes!'

The couple shyly walked across the street, with Wayne's heart thudding as he knew his moment had come: he was going to steal a kiss off the girl he adored. He steered her carefully towards the church, a place that was well known as a local lovers' lane where young sweethearts met for secret snogs.

Said Wayne, 'We went for a walk; we knew we were going to snog. I took her to the back of the church:

it was the first kiss that ever mattered to me; she was special.

'I knew then that we were made for each other, but I was lost for words. Coleen did most of the talking – I think she was shocked at what a fantastic kisser I was!

'I walked her home and I phoned her as soon as I got in and asked her for a proper date. The next day we planned to go out. I'd arranged to meet my friends in town and I was so excited I bought a whole new outfit – a green jumper, jeans and brown shoes.'

The couple went to The Showcase Cinema, a frayed, old-fashioned picture house a short stroll from their homes, just the two of them, to see *Austin Powers: International Man of Mystery*, followed by cheeseburger and chips at a fast-food restaurant close by.

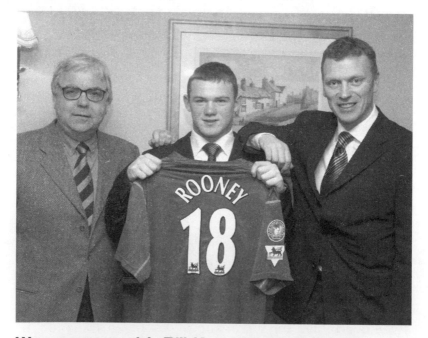

Wayne poses with Bill Kenwright and David Moyes following the signing of his first professional contract on January 17, 2003.

It was their first proper, unchaperoned date and Wayne walked her home, a shy acknowledgement between them that, now, they were officially an item.

'We realised we liked each other more than just mates,' is how Coleen put it. 'When I first started seeing him, I was a bit nervous and we kept it secret. I never told my dad if I kissed a lad, as he is quite protective.'

Wayne was formally introduced to Coleen's family at a christening gathering for her cousin's baby. She said, 'Wayne wore jeans and a shirt – everybody loved him. I expected my dad to be more protective, but he was quite relaxed because Wayne had been coming round so much and he knew his dad from boxing.'

The coals of the sweethearts' passion were ignited, but their romance was forced to slow burn as Wayne's meteoric rise to stardom took off. He was just sixteen, earning £90 a week at Everton, when he hung up his school uniform at De La Salle school for the last time at Easter.

Just seven months later, he became a fully-fledged member of the Everton elite, signing his first professional contract and becoming one of the richest youngsters in world football, earning up to £18,000 a week, including bonuses.

The three-year-deal – the maximum length for a seventeen-year-old – made him the highest-paid teenager in Everton's history, earning the kind of mind-boggling money each week that those from his home turf in Croxteth rarely saw in a year.

The fuse of superstardom had been lit and the football world was fizzing with excitement as Rooney scored goal after sensational goal for the club's youth team. A £2 million endorsement deal with Nike plopped through the letterbox just weeks later and was signed with a trembling flourish of his pen by the disbelieving lad.

Coleen had celebrated her sixteenth birthday on 3 April 2002, just a few weeks before Wayne had left De La Salle school and so certain was he that she'd remain a permanent fixture in his life, he'd had her name tattooed on his right arm.

Again, he'd taken her to the cinema before they enjoyed her birthday outing to Liverpool's trendy 051 club, with Wayne sipping a shandy while she stuck to Coke, taking a taxi back and lingering on the wall near her home, chatting amiably and excitedly about Wayne's prospects, until the front door opened and her mum called her in.

Her parents were strict about time-keeping, anxious that she should prepare for the exacting A-levels she was due to begin at St John Bosco sixth form in September, and determined that what might be no more than a fleeting teenage infatuation should not distract their clever daughter from her studies.

But Wayne already knew that Coleen was the girl for him. He said, 'I'd stopped going out with my mates as much, although I still played football before I saw her every night! I just wanted to be with her.'

As Wayne wandered slowly home, his clockwork mind quietly ticking, he felt a bubble of happiness well inside him and he smiled: he knew that Coleen was the girl he wanted to marry. It was just a matter of time before he'd let her know. It never occurred to him that the whole world would want to know, too.

But that moment, the moment when Wayne would shake the football world to its foundations and become a global superstar, was just around the corner. Destiny would come knocking, first in the momentous signing for his beloved Everton and then, with fairytale unreality, in the form of England manager Sven-Goran Eriksson.

Rooney, instantly promoted to the Toffees' first-team squad and handed the No. 18 shirt previously sported by Paul Gascoigne, took just weeks to smash his way into Everton's record books.

On 24 September, in a bitterly contested match against Wrexham, the teenage powerhouse became Everton's youngest-ever scorer, sent on as a sub to belt home two astonishing goals in the Worthington Cup win.

No time to reflect: Wayne Rooney gets stuck in to training on the very day he signed his professional contract with Everton.

But it was his spectacular last-minute goal against Arsenal a month later that left the football world open-mouthed, drooling at the sheer, audacious brilliance of the boy: a boy still five days short of his seventeenth birthday.

'Wayne Rooney is phenomenal. There's absolutely no doubt about it.'

Paul Gascoigne

It was a goal that saw world-class keeper David Seaman, the England squad's safe pair of hands, left sitting helplessly on his backside: it also saw Rooney become the Premiership's youngest-ever scorer.

An awe-inspiring legend was being carved on the hallowed pitches of England's Premiership clubs and,

Wayne was named the Young Sports Personality of the Year in December 2002 at the star-studded BBC sports awards. The 17-year-old striker was handed the gong by Sven-Goran Eriksson as his manager David Moyes watched on from the audience. Wayne received criticism from a number of papers for chewing gum and leaving the top button of his shirt undone when he collected the award!

just a few months later, the whole world would hear the story. Knock, knock, Sven was calling ...

Rooney was so staggered to be asked to play for England that he immediately assumed the gaffer meant he was up for the Under-21s. But he was wrong. From the very first training session, the rest of the England squad were impressed by Wayne's burgeoning power.

'Well, I got the ball, managed to beat a few players and then chip the goalie,' explained Wayne, as if it were the most obvious thing in the world for a kid of his age to be doing against the best footballers in the country. 'It was one of my first sessions and all the players just looked at me and started to clap.'

'I'm not afraid of the age of 17.'

Sven-Goran Eriksson

'I'm more scared of my mum than I am of Sven-Goran Eriksson!'

Wayne Rooney

His debut match against Australia at Upton Park in February 2003 was a humiliating defeat for England: a 3-1 scoreline to the Socceroos that sent hearts plummeting, especially since the Three Lions were odds-on favourites to win.

But a hero emerged from the ashes of defeat – Rooney, who became England's youngest-ever player at the age of seventeen years and 111 days, had out-performed some of the nation's biggest football names: his place in the galaxy of soccer's greats was already becoming assured.

He'd played alongside his heroes, the men he'd cheered

A nervous-looking Rooney on his debut for England, against Australia.

wildly as a little schoolboy, sitting in the front room of his gran's council house, willing England to victory.

His name was on everyone's lips. Suddenly, the world was his oyster and people were suddenly clamouring to congratulate and celebrate with the newborn star. But there was only one place he wanted to be: back at home, on the proud-as-punch streets of Croxteth and with the girl he loved.

With the thrill of his record-breaking game still coursing through his veins, Wayne dashed back to share his first moments of glory with Coleen; he was dropped off at her parents' home by a friend – an England star he may have been, but he still hadn't passed his driving test.

Later, as twilight blanketed the ragged Croxteth skyline, he shared a bag of chips, a bottle of cola and a kick-about in the street with his mates: it was just an ordinary evening for the extraordinary boy who had the world at his feet.

> **At 17 years and 111 days, Rooney became the youngest player ever to play for England when he came on as a second half substitute in the friendly against Australia on February 12, 2003.**

It would be the last time he'd need to buy his own Coke – within weeks, Rooney had signed up with Coleen to a £500,000 advertising campaign with the fizzy drinks giant: it was a team effort, just like Posh and Becks before them.

And, just a month later, the lad who had worn hand-me-down trainers was revelling in the luxurious surrounds of the England training camp at La Manga. It was a million miles from the caravan in a Welsh holiday park near Rhyl where he'd spent childhood holidays with his cousins; the boys booting their way to glory on a tufted square of sun-baked grass that served as their stadium.

La Manga was a name he knew. It was famous as the base for England's pre-season training and had frequently been linked in newspaper headlines with tales of drunken antics and high jinks among the pampered players.

And here he was, about to join the serried ranks of England shirts at La Manga, with his dream of playing in the Euro 2004 qualifiers just a few weeks from becoming reality.

La Manga, a five-star resort where the scent of money wafted lazily across the manicured lawns, is packed with the kind of exotic luxuries that Wayne had only ever previously brushed up against in the pages of glossy magazines that had been carelessly discarded in the players' lounge at Everton for others to flick through.

It held few mysteries, though. He'd been carefully coached from an early age by the team at Everton's Academy and had then been taken under the wing of Alan Stubbs, a senior club player, who had ensured that the boy from the backstreets was well steeped in the polish that would help him blend in.

But for Coleen, still every inch a schoolgirl, the very thought of setting foot in the place was enough to stir in her the kind of frantic anxiety that any woman feels on her first foray into unknown sophistication, never mind a sixth-form student from the worn-down streets of

Crocky. 'I didn't know what to expect. I was dead scared,' she admits.

She was helped by the fact that the couple's relationship was now a firm fixture. Wayne had been welcomed into Coleen's family, staying at their home overnight to share tender moments with his girl.

Said Wayne, 'Coleen had a TV and video in her

bedroom and we'd go upstairs together to watch things like *Grease* or *Armageddon*. I remember I told Coleen I loved her first. We were watching *Pearl Harbour*, sitting on the sofa at her house. I just told her I loved her; I think the film was a bit of an emotional one and it just came over me!

'Even when I used to go home, which was just down the road, I'd phone her as soon as I got in the door to tell her I was back. Then I'd text her to tell her that I loved her, and I'd often pick her up from school.'

The rock-solid relationship met with the approval of Coleen's mum and dad. They recognised Wayne's serious intent – and their daughter's love for him – and agreed to allow Coleen to make her first trip alone with Wayne, to La Manga.

It would be the first time she had flown alone – Coleen had to sit an English exam on the day the squad flew out and joined her hero a day later. And she was petrified!

She said, 'I rang Wayne and asked him to find out what kind of clothes the women were wearing. I told him to look when they came down for breakfast, but he told me everyone had eaten in their rooms. I was really worried I would take the wrong clothes or not know what to do.'

Just a few months earlier, she'd decked herself out in a simple powder-blue top and white jeans to celebrate her seventeenth birthday with Wayne at the Kung Fu Chinese restaurant in St Helens, five miles away from the council house she still shared with her parents.

Later, a delighted Coleen unwrapped her sweetheart's gift, a £6,000 Marc Jacobs watch, which would soon to be replaced that Christmas with an £18,000 diamond-encrusted, platinum Rolex – *de rigueur* among the glitterati at La Manga.

But now, with her flat, black shoes, short socks, lumpy padded anorak and skin devoid of make-up, Coleen, a rucksack slung across her shoulders, was still the kind of everyday girl who could be spotted at school bus stops across the nation.

She had been relying on her man to come up with the vital information on the wardrobe front. But, like a typical bloke, Wayne couldn't understand what all the fuss was about. Clad casually in a t-shirt and shorts as he roamed the upmarket resort, he still hadn't completed his spy mission by the time a nerve-wracked Coleen was boarding her plane from Britain.

'When I got to the airport, I rang him again to find out and he still didn't know,' she said. 'Luckily, when I arrived, I had bought the right clothes!'

A resourceful girl, Coleen, like her friends, had spent fascinated hours on dreary, rainy days, poring over pictures of the high-maintenance women often found draped on the arms of footballers and pop stars.

An express shopping trip with her mum around the designer stores of Manchester, a short hop from Liverpool and boasting a posh Harvey Nichols, secured the glitzy dresses, sunglasses and the trendy red Burberry bikini that would see her elevated to cover-girl status from the minute she touched down on her sun lounger.

She said, 'My mum rang me to tell me there were pictures of me all over the newspapers. I couldn't believe it – I was dead worried what I looked like in my bikini!'

She needn't have worried. The girl Wayne

Coleen sporting
her red bikini
around the pool
at La Manga.

affectionately called 'Babe' looked gorgeously natural – a refreshing change from the sleekly expensive artifice surrounding her – and was soon the tabloid's darling: her natural curves, dewy young skin and innocent charm quickly elbowed Victoria Beckham off the front pages.

At first, naturally, Coleen was overawed by the world-famous celebrities around her. Surreally, people she'd only ever seen in pictures sat beside her at breakfast, chatting with their families about plans for the day over freshly-baked croissants, at ease and at home in the plush surroundings: Liverpool striker Michael Owen, his baby daughter Gemma nestled in his arms, lounged in the sun with his partner Louise Bonsall, sharing a joke with Wayne; Steven Gerrard, another hero-worshiped Red, and his stunning girlfriend Alex, soaked up the 80-degree heat nearby, teasing the couple with Scouse humour and beginning a bond that would later see him become a pal to

Wayne enjoying a spot of putting on the golf course.

Rooney as the lad sweltered under the unwavering glare of the media spotlight.

Queen bee Victoria offered the hand of friendship, inviting Coleen to spend the day with the girls while the boys sloped off for a game of golf – a first for Wayne but, inevitably, not a last – or to challenge each other at go-karting.

Coleen was soon gossiping away with the rest of them, relaxed in sleeveless t-shirt – the royal blue of Everton, of course – and grey camouflage shorts, as she absorbed the buzz of conversation around her.

'Victoria was chatting away, she was lovely,' said Coleen, 'but I mostly hung out with Steven Gerrard, Jamie Carragher and Michael Owen and their girlfriends, because we're all from Liverpool.'

Alone at night, she snuggled up with Wayne to watch *Only Fools and Horses* on a DVD player, dissecting the day before joining their newfound celebrity friends at dinner.

It was the stuff that dreams are made of: the dreams of little boys and girls who weave feverish fantasies as they fall into a slumber, knowing that, in all probability, they'll never come true. But it seemed as though starlight had fallen on Rooney: it had kissed him while he slept and fairies had plucked his dream for keeping.

'I have to pinch myself to believe what's happened to Wayne,' said Coleen, 'but nobody deserves it more.'

The couple's love affair found breathing space on their first holiday alone, an eye-opening adventure in Miami, lazing on the beach and relaxing in the atmosphere of one of the USA's most celebrated playgrounds. It was there, during blissful sun-drenched days, that love blossomed from courtship to commitment. The prospect of a future marriage hung in the air and, just a week later, the couple joined both their families in the smart Mexican resort of Cancún.

Said Wayne, 'It was a dream holiday compared to those I went on when I was little, but we were young and thought we might be bored on our own, so we

Coleen partners Alex Curran, Steven Gerrard's fiancée, to a charity Childline do in Liverpool

invited our parents to Mexico ... We had a villa and asked Coleen's dad if we could share a room. Coleen was nervous about asking her dad, but it was all right.

'I was a bit awkward at first, too. I didn't know what her dad was going to come out with, because he has a dry sense of humour.

'My parents came as well and they didn't mind at all. They didn't give us the speech about safe sex; we were old enough to know about that.

'Coleen's mum had chatted to her about it, but not in a big lecture kind of way. We knew we wanted to be together and stay together.'

But while affairs of the heart were rapidly developing, the siren song of Rooney's first love was calling and, on 6 September 2003, he answered it with a passion that took the nation's breath away.

Another record toppled, as Wayne became the youngest England player ever to score in a full international, netting the first goal in a 2-1 Euro 2004 qualifier against Macedonia.

Coleen, who had just returned to school to start her A-levels, had to be content with watching her hero shoot his way to victory on the TV at home.

'My whole family were at our house to watch the game,' she said. 'I rang Wayne the day before and said to him, "Are you going to score for me today?" and he said, "Yes!"

'When the goal went in I couldn't believe it. I was rooted to the spot for a moment; I didn't think or do anything. Then, when it sank in, I jumped out of my chair and started screaming and cheering.

Wayne gets to grips with training prior to the game against Macedonia.

'My dad's a Liverpool supporter, but the whole family were leaping around and hugging each other. I was so proud of him.'

Wayne later admitted that he was just as gob-smacked and so blinded by euphoria that he didn't know what to do or where to run after he had scored!

115

Wayne became England's youngest ever goalscorer when on 6 September 2003 he scored in the 53rd minute against Macedonia in England's 2-1 win, aged only 17 years and 317 days.

Rooney may have been just seventeen years old but, with the same certainty that had propelled his football boots, he knew where his romantic heart lay and, just a month later, the soccer star formally proposed to his sweetheart – albeit on the forecourt of a BP garage!

Said Wayne, 'I had the ring made to my design. It's platinum and diamond – I know what she likes. Coleen had tried to interfere, but she made it too complicated!

'I'd picked it up from the jeweller and told her we were going out for a Chinese meal, but we stopped at a BP petrol garage to get money from the cashpoint. When she was getting the cash, I got the box out of my pocket and opened it. She got back into the car and I asked, "Will you marry me?" She was a bit emotional, she said yes and we had a bit of a hug. Asking Coleen to marry me was worse than walking out for England.

'We didn't bother going for that meal. We rang Coleen's mum and told her to get the dinner on and went back to watch *EastEnders* ... Coleen couldn't wait to get back and show everybody her ring. She loves it. When we got there, her mum had put candles on the table. It was really special.

'We'd already discussed getting married a few months earlier. We knew we were only young, but Coleen talked to her mum and she was happy for us. So were my parents when we spoke to them, but I was determined to ask her dad properly.

'I'll never forget the night. We were all sat in the living room watching TV and her dad already knew what was on my mind because her mum had told him. Eventually, after four hours of awkward silence, he finally said: "Haven't you got something to say to me, Wayne?"

'I said, "Can I marry your daughter please?" Then he gave me a big lecture and said, "If you love each other, I give my blessing."

'Then he told me to look after her, but said it was two people from the same area who loved each other and he knew it was right. Finally he shook my hand and her mum started crying.'

Even better, just a few weeks earlier, Wayne had passed his driving test – at his third attempt – and the couple could now seek the privacy they craved away from the bright lights of Liverpool.

Said Coleen, 'If we go out for dinner or out shopping, we get a lot of people coming up to us. So we mostly went to the cinema, because it was dark and no one could see who Wayne was. Even now, we do our shopping at Tesco at 10pm, because we're less likely to see many people. When Wayne passed his driving test it made things a lot easier.

'He was very nervous when he proposed. People may think we are too young, but I don't think we are. It's up to the individual; I know the time is right. He is the person I love and who I want to stay with for the rest of my life. It's not up to anyone else.

'We haven't set a date yet. I actually do feel too young to do that; it is something that is dead special and I want

Wherever Wayne goes he attracts massive attention, even if it's just a trip to the shops in Manchester.

it to be beautiful and really well planned. We can be engaged for years, so there's plenty of time to make wedding plans.'

Wayne, unafraid to wear his heart on his sleeve, said simply, 'She's a nice girl to be around and I wanted to make sure I keep her around.'

Just a few weeks later, Wayne moved in with Coleen's parents after buying his own mum and dad a £470,000 home in Liverpool's upmarket West Derby.

He says, 'Mum and Dad were moving and getting their house sorted, so I moved in with Coleen's parents. I was virtually living there anyway – I spent most evenings at her house!'

By November, the couple were enjoying the kind of high-profile celebrity lifestyle common among the footballing elite: canoodling in a VIP area at a Beyoncé Knowles concert and, later, Coleen waltzing down the catwalk in a red mini-dress, raising cash at a charity fashion show.

Within a few weeks, she had signed up with Wayne's influential agent Paul Stretford, had landed a small part in Merseyside soap *Hollyoaks* and had quit her A-level studies.

Said Coleen, 'I just felt doing A-levels then wasn't right for me. I was getting offered acting parts, but I couldn't take them because of my schoolwork. I'd like to go to drama school, maybe to university, but there's plenty of time to do that. At the moment, I'm just looking after our new home.'

The couple both love kids – Coleen says they'd like a boy and a girl – but, for the moment, they are content to lavish their affection on her seven-year-old sister, Rosie.

Rosie suffers from Rett syndrome, a neurological disorder that means she is slowly losing her ability to perform everyday tasks like eating and walking.

Wayne recently became the youngster's godfather and says, 'I was dead chuffed to be asked. Rosie has stolen my heart ... She's very poorly, but always laughing – Coleen reckons she is always flirting with me. Rosie can't crawl, so I lift her up and put her on the bed and lie next to her and sing her favourite nursery rhymes.'

Coleen said, 'When Rosie comes to our house, it's Wayne she wants: she's dead in love with him – the only rival I've got for his attention.'

Valentine's Day remains special for the couple – it was when the lovebirds finally enjoyed their first night alone in 2004, enjoying chocolates and champagne at Liverpool's Marriott Hotel, a lavishly restored art deco building that was formally an old-fashioned airport terminal.

Said Wayne, 'We were going to a party and, halfway through the night, I asked Coleen whether we should phone her dad and ask whether we could stay out. He said yes, so I booked a room at the Marriott Hotel in Liverpool. We arrived about 1am and there were champagne and chocolates already there. It was a fantastic night: our first full night completely alone together.'

Just a month later, the couple would leave behind the streets of Croxteth to move into a £1.3 million mansion in Formby, a twenty-minute drive from the council estate that had spawned their love – but a lifetime away from their roots.

FIVE

FROM CHIP-SHOP CHIC TO THE CATWALK

IT'S THE PICTURE that would change her life: Coleen, dressed in school uniform, clumpy black heels and a Puffa jacket stared in startled disbelief as a camera flashed in her face.

She was just an ordinary schoolgirl, concentrating on her GCSE exams and hoping that one day she might become a journalist or an actress. Instead, it would be the start of an extraordinary journey that would lead her through the pitfalls of fashion *faux pas*, from chip-shop chic and 'chav' street-style to becoming a glamorous cover-girl, starring on the pages of elite fashion bible *Vogue*.

Today, Coleen's fashion role model is Kate Moss – and she's more likely to be seen wearing the same gear as Kate than slobbing around in tracksuits as she reinvents herself in the most dramatic transformation since Kylie Minogue left Ramsay Street.

Coleen told the *Mirror*, 'When I had a Saturday job in

New Look, I would save up for a new pair of shoes or a top. Most girls are like that. And on my sixteenth birthday, I spent all day in town with my mates and we walked around every single shop. That's the way I have always been.

'Now I've got my own wages coming in for a magazine column, and money from my fitness DVD and all the photo-shoots I do. And yes, Wayne likes to treat me now and again, too. He's generous and likes to buy me things.

'I've always been ambitious and I've always worked hard – I don't just want to be Wayne's fiancée, I want to be me, a person in my own right.

'I left school at seventeen when I was studying for my A-levels because I wasn't enjoying it and wasn't getting the marks I could. I left because I wanted to concentrate on acting, but then things went up the wall because of all the interest in Wayne and me.'

Coleen is fuming that she has been portrayed as a work-shy teenager who fritters away her multi-millionaire boyfriend's money in endless shopping sprees.

She said, 'People say that Wayne pays for everything and I don't work. He used to tell me to forget about it, because to him it's what's on the back pages that counts. But although I'm more confident now and I realise you have to take the good with the bad, it still annoys me when they go on about it.

'I might be seen at the Liverpool boutique Cricket a lot, but that's because it's my favourite shop and it's run by a mate of mine. I always find something I like in Cricket, it's the best shop ever.

'My best buy has been my Gina boots. I wear them all the time, especially over my jeans. I couldn't get a pair of Stella McCartney thigh high boots that Posh wears. I really wanted those, but I like my Gina boots.

'Wayne is not into fashion. When he goes shopping he gets everything in one go, but if he thinks something looks nice on me, he will say, "You look dead nice." If he doesn't like it he'll say, "It doesn't suit you." He hates going shopping. I buy him most of his clothes for birthdays and Christmas,' she told the *Sunday Mirror*.

Coleen genuinely loves fashion and was saving up for designer togs long before she could afford them. She said, 'When you go out in Liverpool, you will always see loads of great-looking girls in lovely clothes ... I used to go shopping with my mum Colette and my auntie and look at everything, even if I came home with nothing but a hair bobble.

'My wardrobe now still contains clothes from Top Shop and Miss Selfridge as well as designer names. I love Top Shop, Gap and H&M, but I love more expensive labels as well. What does my head in is when you buy something expensive and you see a knock-off version down the market the next day.'

Coleen was devastated when she became the target of scornful sneering at her street style, size and insinuations that she was spending Rooney's money faster than he could make it. It culminated in her being crowned 'Queen of the Chavs' and she was voted the most hated girl in Britain. It hurt.

However, instead of going into hibernation, defiant Coleen proved both her resourcefulness and strength by resolving to undergo a dramatic fashion makeover – and to earn her own money. At just nineteen years old, she is already raking in at least £300,000 a year in her own right. Experts declare that she now has the earning potential of more than £1 million a year.

She said, 'I still look at the price tags on everything, especially in designer shops. I know what it's like when money is hard to come by – I worked as a cleaner and also had a Saturday job working in a shop ... I might pick up a nice plain sweater and then I look at the price tag and it's like £295. Why pay that when you can pick up an almost identical one in Gap for £35?'

'I have made some fashion mistakes,' she told *Heat* magazine. 'I'd say my worst one was probably the moon boots. They were a bit much. I think they were probably more suited to the ski slopes than Old Trafford, but I've learned from my mistakes.'

Coleen also ditched her trademark Juicy Couture tracksuits – in public at least – and the Muck Luck boots that had caused so much sneering and, just two months later, she appeared in *Vogue*, the glossiest of glossy fashion mags.

Fashionistas were appalled, but the magazine's editor, Alexandra Schulman, had spotted Coleen's potential after one of her staff bumped into her while she dined with Wayne at a trendy London eaterie during a Valentine's Day treat.

Alexandra, the high priestess of fashion, defended her decision to launch Coleen in the upmarket mag. She explained, 'We had been thinking about who was intriguing at the moment and Wayne Rooney and Coleen's names came up as a couple who were constantly in the news. One of my staff volunteered that she had seen them the previous week having dinner at the Wolseley restaurant in London's Piccadilly. She had

Coleen turns up the glamour at a charity event, sporting diamond earrings.

gone over to see Wayne for his autograph for her son. Coleen had apparently looked sweetly encouraging of this action – he less so.

'Coleen had impressed her as looking prettier and fresher in the flesh than she did in the paparazzi shots we were all so familiar with. Added to that, everybody was interested to hear what Coleen, a previously mute figure, had to say about her portrayal as public enemy number one. That afternoon, the PR team she shares with Wayne were approached.'

But, incredulously, the answer came back no!

Said Alexandra, 'Coleen, although flattered, didn't want to do any publicity. She had been incredibly hurt by all the press comments about her. A fashion star-struck teenager who didn't want to be in *Vogue* didn't really ring true, so I got on the phone to say that, although we understood Coleen might be wary, it was not going to be a hatchet job we were planning in *Vogue* ... and where would she ever have better pictures taken?

'We went backwards and forwards over a few days and eventually a deal was struck. Coleen would be photographed for *Vogue*, but wouldn't talk about Wayne. She would, however, be happy to talk about fashion. She didn't pay us and we didn't pay her, as rumour has claimed.

'Girls such as Coleen (and it has to be said that there aren't many with quite the credit card flexibility she appears to possess) are a relatively recent fashion phenomenon. Twenty years ago, they simply didn't exist, but more awareness of fashion, an increasing interest in designer brands and the massive growth of the 'must-have' item have changed the shopping landscape.

Fashion nowadays is dependent upon sales, not only to the few but to a mass market. The Coleens of this world, with their obsessive interest in the next handbag, or that pair of boots, are an essential part of the fashion industry.

'When she arrived at the London studio to be photographed, she impressed our team with her unmade-up, pony-tailed look. Naturally, she was carrying a Chloe Paddington bag, this spring's wannahave item. Her jeans and pink jacket were given the thumbs up, but the team were more dubious about the hair extensions and white-tipped manicure. It immediately became clear that she was a normal eighteen-year-old with a normal eighteen-year-old's tastes.

'Do I think she is a style icon? Absolutely not, but I also feel that 'style icon' is the most ridiculous and overused phrase of our time. Do I think she is a role model for young girls? No, but neither do I think that the more conventional content of upper-class girls and models are necessarily lifestyle role models.

'I think she is interesting, because she has become famous entirely through the filter of the paparazzi and tabloid press and that, in itself, makes her a phenomenon of our time.

'She hasn't asked for it and she actually pays good money for her shopping, unlike a lot of people in similar positions who expect to be given outfits for free.'

At one point, while Coleen was ridiculed as the Queen of Chav, store lists for advance orders for handbags would halve overnight if she was seen carrying one. Not so these days.

Said Alexandra, 'I recently had lunch with the British managing director of a world famous brand. She had been visiting the company's shops in the north of England where its current range of bags had been a touch slow out of the starting gate. A few days previously, Coleen had been photographed with one of the bags that was credited in the paper as having been sold for £3,500, approximately six times more than its real price.

'Nonetheless, even thinking that the bags were £3,500 a pop, people rang the Manchester store non-stop with orders in the first days after it was shown dangling from Coleen's arm. Doesn't it make *Footballers Wives* look a bit low key?'

Coleen dressed up to the nines and enjoying herself at Ladies' Day at the Grand National, Aintree.

Coleen has been caught between a rock and a hard place with her fashion profile: she had often been ridiculed and rarely been praised until the amazing *Vogue* pictures appeared. Even then, cynics found something to carp about: apparently outraged that a working-class lass with a curvy body should grace the pages of a high-fashion mag.

Coleen told *Vogue*, 'When it comes down to it, I haven't set out to be famous, but I am beginning to feel like I can't win. Sometimes I wonder if I am being punished for something Wayne has done.

'I'm not the person I'm portrayed as – a shopaholic airhead. And there's all this hype, but I didn't go out and seek it ... And I don't understand that 'chav' label. I don't even know what it is supposed to mean. When you see someone in the paper it is so different to real life, isn't it?

'When I read that I was the most hated girl in Britain,

that made me think. So I started thinking about doing more exercise and watching what I eat. If I lose weight from around my face I don't even look like me and I do want to be me.

'Sometimes, when I read what people have said about me it does upset me. Like any teenager, I still cry over my spots, so it can be hard to take criticism just for being me.

'My way of coping is to smile, even when I am feeling rough ... Because my teeth are so white and straight, people are always asking me if I've had them done, but they're totally natural. I just brush them a million times a day to keep them sparkling and I try to remember to smile as much as I can because I think a smile can light up your whole face. Even on days when I'm feeling rough, I do my best to keep a big grin on my face, especially if the paparazzi are lurking.

'I'm not a big fan of lipstick, though. I much prefer lips gloss to make my lips look sexy. Wherever I go, I've always got some Chanel lip gloss in my handbag.'

Coleen, at just 5ft 3in, has lately been voted one of the world's top twenty-five sexiest women in lads' mag *FHM* along with Sienna Miller, Jennifer Aniston and Angelina Jolie. The previous year, she didn't even make the top 100.

The mag's editor, Ross Brown, says, 'She is not doing much wrong in the eyes of men. As soon as the poll opened, she shot straight into the top twenty-five.'

As a result of her new fitness regime – she has shed 10lbs and toned up in the gym – Rooney now has a foxy chick on his hands.

Coleen told *Top Santé*, 'Wayne adores how shapely I am and is forever grabbing me around the waist ... I've always had a shapely waist. I'm a curvy woman and that's just how I like it – and so does he. I'll certainly never become one of those celebrities who becomes really skinny. I just love my curvy bum and hips too much. And my food!

'To show off my curves, I wear lots of 1950s style clothes, like pencil skirts, heels and big belts pulled in at the waist. It's such a good look for shapely girls like me who are proud to show off their curves.

'In the last year or so, my whole body has become really toned – thanks to regular gym workouts – and my stomach is much flatter.

'I reckon exercise is definitely the key to looking good. I just love my food too much to bother to diet. As long as you are sensible, it's easy to stay in shape. I try to eat well most of the time, but I'm only human and I'm still into my Chinese takeaways.

'I think the bit of my body I like best is my shoulders. I absolutely love showing off my sexy shoulders. No matter how much I weigh or how pale I am, I always feel great about my shoulders ... I love showing them off in strapless tops and dresses. I think a
flash of shoulder is far sexier than a flash of cleavage and my shoulders look better than ever at the moment because I'm also doing boxercise classes.

'I'm lucky my skin keeps its colour long after I return from holiday – I hate fake tan, I never use it ... When I want to show off my shoulders, I just sweep some bronzer across them and I'm ready to hit the town.'

Coleen has impressed the fashion world with both her professional approach and down-to-earth manner. On the day she arrived for the *Vogue* shoot, she turned up at 9am on the dot in her favourite James jeans, a pair of

Coleen puts in a smart appearance at the Ariel Fashion Awards.

white Converse Allstars and a Matthew Williamson embroidered cotton kaftan top, clutching that pale beige Chloe Paddington bag bought from her favourite boutique in Liverpool.

She steers clear of the flashiest designer labels, opting for elegant labels like Missoni or Matthew Williamson rather than Gucci or Chanel.

'They're too grown up for me,' she told *Vogue*. 'I recently went out with Wayne to The Ivy, it was dead exciting. Tom Ford from Gucci and Valentino were there – and I just wore a little coral-coloured Temperley dress that I like a lot with a pair of suede boots from Cricket.

'I love accessorising. I've never bought a Prada dress, but the Prada sports shoes are great – I've got a few pairs at home. And I love YSL shoes – I've got three pairs of their strappy sandals. Juicy Couture tracksuits are comfortable to wear during the day, so I still have them.

'I love bags. I saw Heidi Klum with a pink and black Chanel bag, which I loved, so I bought one like it while I was in New York and a cherry Louis Vuitton bag in Sloane Street.

'I pay the full price for everything; I get no special favours. I know some people get stuff sent to them, but I think that would take a lot of the fun out of it – I actually like going shopping and searching things out.

'I like having a blow-out in places like Miss Selfridge – I love their boots – and I've just bought some skinny jeans from Top Shop and a black and white stripey jumper from George at Asda.'

The transformation of Coleen has been little short of a revolution – and that doesn't just apply to her wardrobe.

She's even released her own fitness DVD – *Coleen McLoughlin's Brand New Body Workout.*

She explained to the *Mirror*, 'I was on holiday in Barbados with Wayne when I was photographed by the pool in my bikini. The producers at Universal Pictures spotted my potential and called my agent about doing the DVD. I'd been working out on my own once or twice a week at the gym and it wasn't like I lost loads of weight, but my body shape was different. I'd noticed that I was creeping up from a size ten to a twelve. I was putting weight on my legs, bum and thighs because I was getting too comfortable.

'Universal got me a personal trainer and I started working out three times a week – aerobic workouts – and it made a big difference.

'I started eating more healthily, cutting down on carbs, especially my favourite crisps and chips and eating fruit and nuts instead. I went to a few Weight Watchers classes with my mum and it helped, knowing the calories in everything. Now I'm dead happy with the way I look. I do have a little cellulite, but I don't worry about it. I feel better in myself because I have more positive energy.'

Coleen's workout regime includes Flexibar classes – a piece of equipment that is said to help firm up the wobbliest of wobbly bits. Workouts involve moving the bendy 4ft plastic bar in front or to one side in order to improve the body's core strength. The one-hour Flexibar workouts are tough aerobic exercises that were originally devised by physiotherapists in Germany to help eliminate back pain by building up the muscles in the midriff.

Coleen, however, has ruled out becoming a skinny

'lollipop head' waif like her friend Victoria Beckham – although she finds criticism of Posh hard to stomach.

She continued, 'I get really upset at nasty comments about Victoria. I think, "How can you say these things when you've never even met her?"

'We have girly chats and she's just wonderful – so down to earth. I really love her and anyone who knows her feels the same.'

As every woman can verify, there is always one thing they would dearly love to change about their body and Coleen is no different. She told *Company* magazine, 'I'd like to be taller and have longer legs. I like it when I see girls in skinny jeans wearing flat shoes and their legs look dead nice, so I'd definitely like longer legs ... I get photographed a lot and it can make you self-conscious. I try to ignore the criticism, but you can only ignore it to a certain extent. Sometimes, you just think: "Well, that's me, and you've got to take me for who I am." It's hard if I know I've put on a bit of weight on my legs and, of course, the newspapers always notice.

'I'd be dead embarrassed if I was asked to do a lads' mag shoot just yet, it's just not really me. I'm not a glamour type of girl – I'm more a girls' girl. I'd never say never, but not at the moment.

'I'm still trying to develop my own style. Kate Moss is my fashion heroine and I also admire Cat Deeley's style. She can do dressy and casual really well ... I'm more of a casual girl. I'd rather just go to the shops in my trackies, but I do love getting dressed up for nights out.'

She told *Company*, 'My first ambition in life was to work in the sweet shop next to my house. And then I wanted to be a teacher, but I think everyone wants to be a teacher at some point. Then, I wanted to do drama, then journalism and then it was back to drama again but even as a schoolgirl I always loved fashion. My Saturday job in New Look was dead brilliant because it meant I got fifty percent off – my wages were gone on the first day!

'I also worked as a cleaner with my auntie to earn enough to buy clothes. I saved and saved to buy my first designer top and it came from Cricket, just like now.'

The future looks bright for ambitious Coleen. Aside from the magazine appearances and the fitness DVD, she's already had a walk-on part in *Hollyoaks*, starred in her own documentary on Channel Five and is bidding for a role in *Coronation Street*.

Her big dream is to rival *Doctor Who* star Billie Piper, twenty-three, and fellow Liver bird Jennifer Ellison, twenty-

Coleen on holiday in Majorca.

two. She said, 'I want to be an actress, but I want to be a proper actress, to learn things properly at drama school. I've been offered quite a lot of parts, but I'm not ready and the role has got to be right for me.

'I've been taking acting and dancing lessons since I was seven and I've always wanted to act – I was going to study the performing arts. The way I see it, there's plenty of time for me to do that still ... I want to be able to hold my own in the acting world. And I won't really be able to do that without a proper, professional grounding. That means drama school.'

She aims to silence the critics who have claimed that she funds her lavish lifestyle through handouts from her fiancé. She said, 'Work is really important to me. I don't want to be a Stepford Wife or a footballer's wife. I want an identity of my own.'

Coleen is also contemplating launching her own fashion range and is in talks to lend her name to everything from make-up to perfume. But she's cautious and careful about her own branding: 'It's got to be dead classy,' she says. 'I love stylish clothes – and diamonds. I love wearing diamonds. I feel dead classy.'

It's just as well. She recently turned up at the National Television Awards in a 1950s vintage dress and £1 million worth of diamonds borrowed from high-class jeweller Chopard. It was proof, if proof were needed, that Coleen had finally been accepted among the glitterati.

She said, 'The diamonds were stunning. They were heart-shaped and I picked them because I am in love ... I felt really precious because they were worth £1 million – it meant I had to have a bodyguard with me all night.

'I was modelling myself on Audrey Hepburn. I think she had so much class and I really love her ... I think the 1950s style is so much more elegant and even though it is very trendy right now, for me it will never be unfashionable because that is the style I really admire.'

But Coleen's own greatest admirer is Wayne. And their love-match is as touching as it is without pretension.

Forever Blue? Evertonian Rooney's sparkling eyes give no hint of the future as he collects the BBC Young Sports Personality of the Year award in 2002.

Wayne takes his
football very seriously,
but not to the exclusion
of enjoying a good
laugh, *(above)* during
training ahead of an
England international
and *(right)* even on the
subs' bench for
Manchester United.

Wayne Rooney shakes the hand of Sven-Goran Eriksson, the England manager who gave him his international debut at the tender age of only 17.

Above: Rooney strikes
again! This time against
Denmark in November 2003.

Right: After breaking his
metatarsal at the quarter
finals of Euro 2004, it was
not until the autumn that he
was able to resume his
glittering England career.
Here he storms into space
against Wales, showing his
considerable physical
strength and composure.

Above: Fiancée Coleen McLoughlin – childhood sweetheart turned glamourpuss and beach bunny.

Below left: Wayne's set to be one of the highest earners in world football. Sponsorship from sports companies such as Nike earn him millions.

Below right: The world's greatest young footballer at the FIFPRO World XI Player Awards in September 2005 – a huge accolade for a 20-year-old.

Man of the Match, Wayne proudly holds his award after helping his team win the
Carling Cup in 2006 – his first senior prize.

Above: The deadly England strike partnership has worked before – here Rooney celebrates his goal against old rivals Argentina, with Owen in the background. Can it work again?

Below: Rooney at the end of the line for England, but still a key component in his nation's footballing dreams for a long time to come.

Wayne Rooney with the FIFA World Cup Trophy. Is this the closest Rooney will ever get to world football's most coveted prize?

SIX

BETTER THAN THE BRAZILIANS

'People think that Brazil are unbeatable, but they are not. Their defence is nowhere near as strong as their attack and if you look at their record, they have only won the World Cup once in Europe ... and that was as far back as 1958. Whenever Brazil have lifted the trophy it has been on a different part of the football planet. England have to realise that this shows Brazil's life becomes difficult whenever they have to play in Europe and the same will happen in Germany.'

Sven-Goran Eriksson

If Wayne Rooney were to come out of the World Cup as a winner and be viewed as the best player on the planet, then he will have to worry about one monumental factor other than a speedy return from injury: the boys from Brazil.

The Boys from Brazil, seen here lining up before the World Cup quarter final match with England on June 21, 2002. Brazil won 2-1.

There is no doubt that, given a healthy restoration of fitness, the Croxteth Kid can return from Germany acknowledged as the greatest player in the world. That's not just my view, but that of the greatest names in the game, ranging from the late, great George Best to German legend Franz 'The Kaiser' Beckenbauer.

And if he plays like he has done all season and avoids any further injury, then it is a distinct possibility that not only will he be the player that they will all be looking up to, but that England could well become the world champions.

The doubters rubbish it. They like to convince themselves that no English player, or even a European player, can be as good as a Brazilian. I think that the reverse is the case. I don't think that any current

Brazilian player is as good as Wayne Rooney. They don't have the breadth, the vision or the sense of playing within a team that makes the Englishman so special.

Brazil have a fearsome array of players, including four outstanding forwards, but that shouldn't dismay the English, now or in the future. It certainly doesn't worry Wayne Rooney. Speaking on behalf of his keyed-up compatriots, he told the *News of the World*, 'The World Cup is the biggest tournament any of us will ever play in and we have a squad that can go all the way. The nation is behind us and we want to deliver ... This is a golden generation for English football and we know we all have to step up to the plate if we are going to win. But we have the ability and we do not fear anyone.

'Brazil are probably the best team in the world at the moment. We know it will be tough if we do play them, but we will stand up, give our all and make sure we are better than them on the day. There is a feeling that we owe them one after the last World Cup in Japan. I have

'Kaiser' Franz Beckenbauer, the head of the World Cup 2006 organising committee, said, 'I have never before seen a player like Rooney.' Beckenbauer, who won the World Cup both as a captain and a coach, went on: 'When I look at Rooney the word "superstar" comes to mind. When I look at him, what I see is a natural scorer, a real finisher. A very, very good one. I can't think of anybody I have seen like him. He is a unique talent.'

spoken to the lads and I know that those who were there are still hurting about it.

'Ronaldinho has said that we can get to the final and that would be a dream for me. To play against Brazil would be brilliant and to get to a World Cup final and then face the team acknowledged as the best in the world would be the greatest challenge ever. As long as we get to the final I won't care who we play. Of course, I would love to score in the final, but I won't be bothered as long as we win.'

In the run-up to the competition, as the domestic season drew to a close, the United sensation had no worries at all about the expectations slowly building upon his shoulders. He added, 'The fact that people expect so much of me is not a burden. I don't feel that it is a weight. In fact, I quite enjoy the sensation. Of course, it's a real buzz to be talked about alongside the likes of Ronaldinho, David Beckham and other big stars, but I try not to think about it. The European Championships were very good for me until we got knocked out by Portugal after I broke my foot. I was gutted. Now I want to carry on where I left off.

'It's a big advantage having the finals in Germany. I know how some of the lads struggled in the Far East and this is probably our best chance in a long time.'

With manager Sven-Goran Eriksson now certain to leave his England post after the finals, to be replaced by Steve McClaren, Rooney spoke for the squad when he told the *News of the World* that the players want to win it for their outgoing boss.

He said, 'There is a feeling we should win the cup for Sven. He is a great manager. All the players like him and respect him and, more importantly, he trusts us. He treats us as professionals. He believes that we know what is best for ourselves – he is good like that ... He has been so unlucky in the way we have gone out of tournaments in the past. Hopefully we can win it and if there is anybody who deserves success it is him.'

Not everybody would agree that it was only bad luck that led to England's exit in Japan. Sven has been criticised ever since for a perceived inability to motivate his players to hang on to a 1-0 lead and to rally them when the Brazilians hit back in a quarter-final that England seemed destined to win.

It has always been the cornerstone of any criticism against Sven: that he has not shown enough passion in the dugout to fire the bellies of his players in the sort of way demonstrated, for example, by Martin O'Neill.

Rooney has duly acknowledged the threat of the South Americans and the threat they pose to England's ambitions. But unlike most people in this country, he is neither paralysed by fear at the sight of a yellow, green and blue strip and nor does he think they are invincible.

We are constantly reminded of the talents of Ronaldo and Robinho (both Real Madrid), Adriano (Inter Milan) and Ronaldinho (Barcelona). They are four fine footballers. They have great individual skills, but could any man in the street name one outstanding Brazilian defender? Most people would probably say Roberto Carlos, another Real Madrid player, but in fact he's more like a winger than a full-back.

And we should remember that while the above form a fearsome attacking force, it would be very difficult for any manager, even in charge of Brazil, to play more than two of them at any one time.

And under close examination, they each lack one or more of the characteristics that make Wayne Rooney a more complete player. Ronaldo is on the downward slope of his career. As each month goes by, you get the impression that he has to work harder and harder to keep on top of his fitness.

Adriano is a player who has not yet settled down to make his mark with any one club. At twenty-three, he is already into his second spell at Inter Milan after a carousel ride around Italian foootball that took in Fiorentina and Parma.

A kid from the slums of Rio de Janeiro, he burst onto the scene as a seventeen-year-old with Flamengo. He seems to be a better player at international level than for his various clubs, having scored twenty-one times for Brazil in twenty-eight appearances.

His big problem is that his best position seems to be in the role that Ronaldinho already plays and it is a bit unfortunate to be the understudy to the World Player of the Year. He was, though, the subject of one of the most amusing pieces of commentary dialogue in the history of the broadcast game. The man at the microphone, Beni Thurnheer ,said, 'Adriano says that his role models are Kaka and Jesus. That's Kaka of Milan and Jesus of Nazareth.'

Ronaldinho is outstanding for Barcelona, is probably the best purely attacking player in the world and, therefore, the worthy recipient of his award as the FIFA World Player of the Year. But it doesn't matter how good he and the others are in their respective positions. What none of them can do is operate comfortably in more than one area of the pitch.

Ronaldinho, often acclaimed as the best attacker in the world, and a huge threat to any opposition's goal.

With Ronaldinho clearly established as one of the very best, the Brazilian boy who will be trying to stake his claim as the new sensation at the World Cup will undoubtedly be Robinho.

Many say he will emerge from the tournament as the new world sensation, in much the same way as Rooney did following his performances in Portugal 2004. Others, like me, hope that Rooney gets the opportunity to eclipse him on the highest stage. Rooney already has the experience of dominating a major international competition and he arrives in Germany off the back of an outstanding domestic season, albeit one concluded with a broken foot. In contrast, the Brazilian has had a miserable time at Real Madrid. He did pick up, as did most of the Bernabeu squad, after manager Luxemburgo disappeared just before Christmas, but he did not have a consistent season.

And as for him being a surprise package rather than an established star like Rooney, the problem with that is that he is already known to top defenders because of his high-profile domestic role. Remember, Rooney was playing for struggling Everton when he burst onto the world scene. None of the world's great defenders, most of whom play in Europe, had ever played against him.

Robinho, born Robson De Souza, emerged from a dusty Brazilian backstreet and started playing football on the beach with pieces of discarded fruit found in the gutters around his basic home. Anything would do – an orange or even a plum – as long as it was something that was vaguely round and that he could keep up in the air.

According to his mother, he was the easiest child to buy presents for. All he ever wanted out of the meagre family budget was a new football – or, if possible, a real pair of football boots.

He has already been compared to the original Brazilian legend, even by Pelé himself, who said, 'He reminds me of me. The first time I saw him I got goose-bumps. I almost cried. His dribbling was just devastating, so was the simplicity with which he controlled the ball.'

Like a lot of youngsters who show outstanding promise before they have been developed as a footballer, Robinho was physically slight. One of the Santos coaches recommended that he should be released because he was so frail that he would never be able to handle the rigours of the professional game.

Pelé said, 'He hardly had the strength to strike the ball. He looked so under-nourished that I asked his parents if he suffered from some kind of anaemia.'

Like Rooney, Robinho became the teenage sensation of his football-mad country. But he did not make a first-team debut until he was eighteen, two years behind his English counterpart. However, when it came, he stayed in the team and helped Santos to win their first domestic title in twenty-one years.

His distinctive trademark was one that has been perfected by many Latin players over the decades: the step-over. The Brazilians call it the '*pedalada*' and, in a country where entertainment is just as important as victory, the more *pedaladas* you can execute during a game, the more attention you are going to receive.

We have seen many overseas players in England in recent years using the step-over to try and bamboozle defenders. Manchester United's Portuguese star,

Cristiano Ronaldo, is probably the greatest exponent of it in our game.

But according to Robinho-watchers, his ability to go forward at alarming pace and perform umpteen step-overs at a time makes him the foremost *pedalada* wizard of the world.

He is best remembered in Brazil for a mesmerising performance against Corinthians that gave Santos their title. Running at a hapless defender, Robinho unravelled

Robinho shows his skills against South American neighbours Chile.

his opponent's brain by stepping-over the ball eight times before he was dragged down in the penalty area. Not to be outdone by the frustrated full-back, he stepped up and scored from the spot.

It was his defining moment in Brazil. He told *Four Four Two* magazine: 'It was funny really. The defender just kept backing off. I'll never forget it. After the match the fans were crying. There were 70,000 people going crazy.'

On another occasion, he was actually booked for doing too many step-overs. The referee's logic was that he was provoking the wrath of defenders by showing them a lack of respect. He had to try and dissuade the boy from continually demonstrating his extraordinary skills in case he became subject to violent retaliation!

Apparently, one opponent had already told him, 'Start showing more respect or somebody will break your legs.' Robinho responded by saying, 'It's not lack of respect. It's just what I've always done. I'm trying to score goals.'

It became increasingly obvious that the boy was always going to end up in Europe. The worldwide network of scouts and agents, employed by every big club in England and the continent, had been alerted to his special talent.

His development had been typical of his background. He said, 'We weren't rich, but that did not matter. I was very happy because I was always playing football – on the beach, in the street, in fact anywhere ... I played indoor five-a-side football and, because it is quicker and closer, it helped me develop my technique. We played football for fun back then, so when I switched to eleven-a-side, I just started taking people on.'

As he got older, coaches started turning their attention to how skinny he was. He was put on a 'beefing-up' diet several times, being fed Argentinian meat three times a day. But it hardly made any difference to his physical appearance. Less worried than anybody else about this was Robinho himself. He felt perfectly capable of playing despite his lack of bulk. He said, 'If you play intelligently, there's no player, however big, that can catch you.'

As his presence grew in South America, he attracted accusations of being a showboater. He was accused of the same sort of failings that are levelled at Rooney's United team-mate Ronaldo, the namesake of Robinho's Brazilian team-mate.

He was very good at dribbling and successive step-overs to bamboozle defenders, but his coaches wanted him to be aware of his team responsibilities. Although the step-over routine can make a player look like a world-beater in front of a clod-hopping defender and can turn a crowd delirious, it can also often be frustrating for team-mates.

When Robinho's coaches could see their wonder boy going down the same track, they acted. They started drilling into him the need to interact with the other players, to pass when appropriate, to create opportunities to cross the ball and to learn how to shoot on sight. It resulted in him upping his goal tally in 2004 to twenty-one goals in thirty-seven games and it was only then that he obtained his first international cap, at the age of twenty.

Rooney was first capped at seventeen and, as a result, he played in and made a huge impact on Euro 2004. Robinho still has to make his presence felt at an international tournament. But, nevertheless, he had become *the* football icon of the southern hemisphere and big-name admirers were queuing up to deliver the plaudits. 'A walking portrait of Brazilian football,' said the legendary Zico. 'Unbelievable,' according to Maradona and, according to Roberto Carlos he is 'the new Garrincha'.

Inevitably, he was to follow the path from South America to continental Europe. At first, it seemed as though he was heading for Barcelona. He told the Spanish magazine *Don Balón*, 'Although I love watching Ronaldo, I want to play at Barcelona. When I heard that Barcelona were interested I was really happy. I'd love to bring Barcelona fans joy. Their philosophy of football is mine, too. They play the beautiful game. Players like Romario, Ronaldo and Rivaldo all played well there and, of course, there is Ronaldinho.'

But despite this apparent enthusiasm, he eventually ended up at Real Madrid. The chiefs at the Bernabeu appointed Wanderley Luxemburgo, the coach who had brought Robinho to maturity at Santos, as the new boss of Real Madrid. That sealed Robinho's future. Knowing that he would have the opportunity to work with the coach he trusted most – and the one he called affectionately 'the professor' – he decided to opt for Barcelona's arch-rivals.

He said, 'Madrid are the greatest club in the world and everybody knows that. I have to go to Madrid because when I am there I will be able to focus exclusively on my football.'

His path to the Spanish capital was anything but smooth. He exhibited the same dogged determination to move on that was characteristic of Wayne Rooney's move from Everton to Manchester United. When he thought that his club, Santos, were standing in the way of his dream move, he refused to train. Showing great determination, he stood up against the pressure from club president Marcelo Teixeira and ignored a public campaign to keep him, led by the country's leader, President Lula. Eventually a £15 million move went through and he moved to Madrid.

He admitted that he wished it had gone smoother, saying, 'I love Santos, but it was time to move on. I had to be in Europe: only there can I become the greatest footballer in the world ... My departure was problematic and the process was definitely not ideal. The Santos president wanted me to stay, but my mind was in Europe. I just couldn't help it. The negotiations were tough and I made some bad decisions – like skipping training – but it all got resolved eventually. I left the club by the front door. It's a joy to play for Madrid, the best place for my career. I had offers from Arsenal, PSV, Inter and Benfica, but none of them could offer what Madrid could.'

One of the offers, of course, was the fact that the boy was joining the most 'Brazilian' Real Madrid team of all time, although the links between the club and the country go back to the all-conquering team of the 1950s.

Robinho said, 'I'll miss home, but I'll be joining a club where I have friends. They are all here – Ronaldo, Roberto Carlos, Julia Baptista and Luxemburgo. I aleady have a great relationship with the Professor [Luxemburgo]. I have no fears about missing my family with whom I am in touch all of the the time ... I know it will not take me long to adjust. Madrid is beautiful and the people are very warm. I feel like I actually could be at home. I am so delighted to be here.'

The feeling about being there was clearly mutual.

Robinho finds himself in a very similar situation, in terms of aspirations, to Rooney at Manchester United. Probably the two biggest clubs in the world, they have suddenly found themselves in an unusual time-warp in the modern era where they are not guaranteeing their fans silverware every season – or at the worst, every other season.

As Rooney arrived at Old Trafford, United were losing more and more components of the team that had given them a golden era from the start of the Premiership in 1992 until their last title in 2003. They also won the FA Cup in 2004.

Rooney nearly tasted glory when he lined up in the FA Cup final in 2005 against the old enemies Arsenal: he was Man of the Match in a game that United dominated before the Reds eventually lost on penalties.

And in his second season at Old Trafford, the firebrand has once again missed out on the big trophies: the Champions League, the Premiership title and the FA Cup will all have passed Rooney by in 2005–06.

Although nobody was going to admit it when he went to Old Trafford, he went with the huge expectation of the management and the fans that he was going to revive a United team that had suddenly lost its clear focus on where the trophies were and how to make sure that they gobbled them up.

One major concern to Sir Alex Ferguson in the latter part of his glorious reign has been that his team have not become a European threat season after season as Madrid had been in the previous decade and arch-rivals Liverpool had been in the 1970s and '80s.

A knife was twisted into that particular wound when Liverpool, against everybody's expectations other than those of their own fans, won the top European trophy again in 2005 in the most dramatic final ever seen. They came back from a 3-0 half-time deficit to AC Milan to win the trophy after extra-time and penalties and took their total of triumphs in the competition to five against Manchester United's two.

Things had not gone smoothly at Old Trafford since David Beckham had left the club – ironically, for Real Madrid – after helping United to another Premier League title in 2003: one which may well turn out to be the last of the Ferguson era.

Rooney was handpicked to be the catalyst for a new age of glory. But it soon became clear that even a boy of Rooney's talents could not single-handedly put everything right in a team that was, to use that ghastly phrase, 'in transition'.

United were having problems in midfield. The power-pack of the team in its heyday was David Beckham, Paul Scholes, Nicky Butt, Ryan Giggs and Roy Keane. Beckham and Butt had gone and Scholes hit a mysteriously prolonged spell of poor form after retiring from international football.

But the biggest blow to the stability of the team came less than halfway through Rooney's second season, when Roy Keane and the club fell out and he departed for Celtic. The club knew that he was probably in his last season, but had hoped that he would see the campaign out while they made the necessary moves for a replacement.

Not only was Keane regarded as the heartbeat of the United team, the powerhouse around which everything spun, he was also regarded as Sir Alex Ferguson in disguise.

So when the two men fell out before the start of Rooney's second season, it had a greater effect than if it had been any other member of the squad. Keane didn't like the idea of a pre-season training camp abroad being open to wives and families. As far as he was concerned that was like taking your kids to work.

Three months into the season, after United had entered a lull, Keane, who was injured at the time, started publicly to dish out critical advice to the team.

While in the past this sort of behaviour appeared to have had the 'blind-eye' blessing of boss Ferguson, these new attacks on team-mates were becoming more bitter than they had ever been before.

Keane was acquiring a reputation of being too much of a loose cannon for his own good ... and for that of the club. So concerned were the coaches, they asked their own cable TV station, MUTV, to be vigilant when it next came to interviewing Keane.

When that interview took place, it was so explosive and critical that the MUTV producers decided to refer it back to the club and Ferguson. It was immediately canned, but the contents of the interview inevitably leaked out and caused a huge row. Shortly afterwards, the long-standing skipper and United parted 'by mutual consent'.

Around about the same time, Paul Scholes, rated by

Wayne relaxes and shares a joke with his Man Utd team-mates during training.

many as the finest pure footballer in Britain, suffered a mysterious double-vision problem just as he was coming back into top form.

Sir Alex was struggling with a lack of pace and persuasion in midfield, trying to plug the gap by moulding Alan Smith, bought as an attacker, into the job. Even Rio Ferdinand was played as a holding midfield player when United walloped Wolves 3-0 in the FA Cup after which hysterical headlines demanded that Rio should take up the same role for England in the World Cup.

It was no wonder then that, within this footballing kaleidoscope, it was difficult for United to determine Wayne Rooney's best position: it all seemed to depend on the strength of the other players available for each match.

It's not just that Rooney *can* play in more than one position; he actually *does* play in at least two different positions, no matter where his manager asks him to start. There isn't another player who pulls on a pair of boots today who can make such an overall contribution to a game.

Colin Harvey, his youth coach at Everton, has always believed that he is an out-and-out striker. That was probably born out of the fact that Harvey, who made his debut as a teenager in Milan's San Siro stadium, was in charge of him when he was a goal-scoring machine.

Rooney used to play in teams full of boys who were two or three years older than him, but he was still able to score record-breaking numbers of goals throughout his schoolboy years. But as he has got older, it has become clear that his talents are so extensive that he is just as able playing behind a single forward or two forwards, because he has the vision to be able to supply killer balls as well as create his own goals.

He seems as comfortable setting up chances for his team-mates as he does in scoring himself. And he also looks just as pleased by 'assisting' as he does by finishing the job with his own feet. (By his own admission, he has to improve the quota of goals he scores with his head.)

He is also brilliant when he runs at defences from deep; he does not score many goals inside the six-yard box. He is much more likely to get himself on the end of a one-two that takes him into the area, having perhaps started the move on the halfway line.

> **Wayne's flat-out sprint has been measured at 9.7 metres per second – which is not too far off the pace of an Olympic sprinter whose averages are often just over 10 metres per second!**

Or, alternatively, he could be lashing the ball into the back of the net from way out. He needs very little back-lift to generate such power in his shot that, if one of his cannonballs is on target, it has become a lost cause for a goalkeeper.

Then, of course, there is his ability to fool goalkeepers with a lob, to pulverise them with a volley from 30 yards or to leave them stranded with a deftly-struck free-kick.

Managers find themselves in the position of a medieval monarch at a feast: undecided whether to start with the beef, venison or wild boar, whether to wash it down with beer, wine or mead and then to follow it with brie, camembert or stilton. The possibilities are endless.

One theory about Wayne Rooney is that his brain works as well as that of Einstein – the most famous physicist in modern history.

The wild-haired Einstein came up with the conclusive theory of general relativity and refined thinking on quantum theory. His work contributed towards the development of the atom bomb and many other scientific breakthroughs of enormous importance.

The reason that Rooney has been compared to such an illustrious academic is because of his ability to work out angles, speeds and velocities so quickly and to be able to send a ball exactly where he wants it to go.

In a split second, his brain has to assess a number of different calculations. He has to take into account the fact that there may be two players in the way of a

Albert Einstein, no doubt working out how to strike a ball as effectively as Rooney.

straight shot, so he might want to curl it. Or there could be a particularly strong wind whipping through the stadium, thus needing him to make an allowance for the direction in which the wind is going.

One of Britain's most eminent mathematicians has figured out the complex calculations that Rooney would have to make to score a goal.

'The only subject I liked at school was maths; it's the only GCSE I sat.'

Wayne Rooney

Marcus du Sautoy, Professor of Mathematics at the University of Oxford and Fellow of Wadham College, has worked out scientifically how Rooney achieves one of those spectacular volleyed goals like the one he scored against Newcastle at Old Trafford.

For the purposes of the England team at the World Cup, the academic says we should imagine Beckham crossing a ball that results in a perfectly timed volley by Rooney to score a goal.

The professor says that the young footballer has to solve not one, but three, complicated equations to judge the flight of the ball as it comes flying into the box. Mathematically it is represented like this:

$$y = \left(\tfrac{v}{u}\right)x - \left(\tfrac{g}{2u^2}\right)x^2$$

$$F_D = C_D pAv^2/2$$

$$y'' + akxy' + by' + cy = g$$

The first equation, after Galileo, determines the height of the ball given its starting velocity when it leaves the foot of Beckham. Obviously, Rooney needs to solve this quadratic equation to know where the ball is going to land, so that he can volley it before it touches the ground.

But there also are some complications he needs to factor in. The second equation controls the drag factor of the ball, which changes the ball's velocity as it flies through the air.

The smooth surface of the ball has a strange effect, causing the drag to be very small at first and

then, suddenly, towards the end of its flight, the drag suddenly kicks in, slowing the ball dramatically. It is quite counter-intuitive and has caught out many a goalie.

Thirdly, what about that wicked spin that Beckham may have put on the ball? That's controlled by the third equation – the boomerang equation – a second-order differential equation.

Having worked out the flight of the ball, Rooney needs to solve the equations all over again to find the most efficient path from his foot to the goal while avoiding any obstacles, such as a defender, on the way.

When he strikes an unstoppable volley on target ,Rooney's brain is therefore working on complex physical phenomena which can be modelled mathematically, all at fractions of a second's speed and executed with perfect timing.

There's no doubt about it – the boy's a genius.

And Rooney clearly doesn't believe that his responsibilities for either his club or his country end at just scoring or providing chances up front. What is amazing about the boy is that he likes tackling other players. When did you ever see Bobby Charlton or Gary Lineker – currently England's two highest-ever scorers – throwing themselves enthusiastically into a challenge? Hardly ever.

George Best did it regularly. It is a mark of exceptional players that they want to be involved in every aspect of the game and Best was indisputably the greatest player that Britain has ever produced.

BETTER THAN THE BRAZILIANS

When did we ever see a Brazilian player tackle back? When did we see a boy from the Copocabana who was happier to be supplying balls to the forwards than knocking them in himself? Can the man in the street name any Brazilian defenders? Vaguely. Cafu, maybe?

Great players sometimes stand out in average teams, but more often they become even greater players by being part of a team of highly talented individuals. This has happened often in the great Brazilian teams of the past when otherwise-average players like Rivelino became better as a result of playing alongside true greats like Pelé and Jairzinho.

If he can make it there, Rooney will be both: he will be one of the most talented individuals at the competition, but he will also benefit from the fact that he is surrounded by other truly world-class players.

Steven Gerrard has a claim to be the best midfield player in the world, and one of the few players who can challenge him for that title is his England team-mate, Chelsea's Frank Lampard.

John Terry, also of Chelsea, will reach the peak of his abilities at Germany 2006 and his club's defensive record proves that he must be one of the outstanding defenders in the world. At the heart of Chelsea's defence, and as a vocal and motivational captain, he routinely performs without making any errors and marshals those around him so that they know what is expected of them.

Ashley Cole is a raiding full-back who plays like a Brazilian and is really an extra attacker in disguise. Michael Owen has one of the best goal-scoring records in the world at international level.

Rooney and Owen – the leading attackers in England's youthful and talented lineup.

But it may well be the performances of Rooney that will determine the eventual home of the World Cup trophy in early July. And mentally he is ready for the ultimate challenge of seeing off the Samba Boys from Sugar Loaf Mountain.

'England have a lot of players who can help us win the World Cup. Our squad is very good now – it's even better than the one from 2004.

He continued: 'My main target has to be winning the Premiership with United. As a kid that is the competition that I always dreamed of. World Cups were too far away in those days to dream about.'

And then, in the understated fashion with which he is becoming increasingly familiar, he added, 'But winning the World Cup – that would be pretty good, too.'

SEVEN

ALL THE WORLD CUP'S A STAGE

ROONEY IS IN an elite class of footballers that can be described as the best in the world. He recently named the four men who he believed are the outstanding forwards of this generation and who would challenge for headlines and goal totals in Germany. They each combine pace, exquisite skill, timing and a deadly eye for goals.

RONALDO

United fans do not need reminding about the Brazilian striker who has twice been voted the World Footballer of the Year. In April 2003, he scored a hat-trick that ended the English club's European ambitions that year. His form that night was so sparkling that even though the United faithful were stunned by the defeat, they stood and cheered the Real Madrid striker off the pitch. The *Galácticos* were the reigning European champions at the time and looked set to retain their trophy following their scintillating display. But they were ejected from the competition by Monaco and have not won the trophy since. At the end of that season, David Beckham moved to Madrid. Many thought that he

would be the spark to reignite Real's superiority but, in fact, it was the start of an unusual barren spell for the most successful European side ever, both at home and abroad and that night of hat-trick glory in Manchester is now seen as the pinnacle of Ronaldo's career, which seems to have been in decline ever since. He has fought a battle with his weight throughout his professional career and, recently, cruel newspaper headlines have dubbed him 'MAC Ronaldo', alluding to the fact that he's very partial to a hamburger and suggesting that, perhaps, he's been eating far too many of them. Nevertheless, he has been at the apex of world football at both club and international level for a decade.

However, many believe that we are waiting for the entrance of a new superstar to take his place – and that superstar may well be Rooney. The Brazilian, who formerly played for Madrid's arch-rivals Barcelona, is in danger of being shown up in both pace and stamina. What's more, there are question marks as to whether he will even start for the Samba Boys, bearing in mind that they have three other world-class forwards in

Ronaldinho, Robinho and Adriano, all of whom are younger and none of whom have a weight problem.

THIERRY HENRY

Providing that Henry stays at Arsenal, the debate for the immediate future in English football will be whether he or Rooney holds the mantle of top player in the Premiership. Henry's brilliance needs no introduction. He is a player who can turn a stadium to uproar or silence within a few seconds with his massive range of skills. He can take brilliant free-kicks or he can bamboozle three defenders at a time on a shimmying run down the left or right with a burst of speed that leaves players trailing in his wake. Unlike Rooney, though, his career almost stalled before it had really started.

The Frenchman was bought by Juventus, but could not command a first-team place, as the Italians were unable to unwrap his multitude of skills. But Arsène Wenger demonstrated once again why he is regarded as the finest spotter of talent in the game when he made a low-key approach for him. The Italians didn't really want to sell him because they thought that he was a useful squad player and the Arsenal boss was slowly forced to keep upping his offer – not fast enough to alert Juventus to the fact that Henry was potentially one of the world's great players, but fulsome enough to secure his man. Wenger paid £11 million to get him to Highbury, a sum that raised many eyebrows at the time. That figure now looks cheap and it would probably cost a club three times that to secure the services of the French striker. He has become Arsenal's virtuoso performer, a monolith of a player in a team of giants

Arsenal favourite and
constant dangerman
Thierry Henry.

who have mopped up domestic honours. But what Arsenal couldn't do, even with Henry, was to make any sort of worthwhile imprint on the Champions League until the 2005-06 competition.

Henry forms a part of the Rooney folklore in that he was playing for France in the opening game of Euro 2004 when England lost to two late goals. David Beckham had earlier missed a penalty in the Stadium of Light in Lisbon. The penalty had been won after Wayne Rooney had burst into the area with the ball at his feet and run at the French defence. He was up-ended and England had the opportunity to go 2-0 up. Had Rooney been on the international scene for a little bit longer, he may well have demanded to take the spot-kick himself, but that was the job of the England skipper who, unfortunately, fluffed his shot and left England vulnerable to the French come-back. Henry and Rooney clash on a regular basis in the Premiership and have spoken very highly of each other. Henry admits to being a big admirer of the Croxteth Kid and said, 'Apart from his obvious skills, he plays with his heart.'

ANDREI SHEVCHENKO

The boy born into a peasant family in the communist USSR of the Cold War days could never have imagined as a youngster that he would one day straddle the world stage and bring so much light into people's lives. He was brought up in the closed community that was the Soviet-bloc and is now a national star for his country, Ukraine – a nation that did not even exist when he was born. Although footballers, like all outstanding athletes in the old Russian system, were privileged members of society – they were dubbed heroes of the Soviet Union – they were still nevertheless prisoners within their own country. Had the USSR not crumbled, it is unlikely that we would ever have seen the skills of the AC Milan hit-man more than a few times a year, and only then in European competition.

However, as a child footballing prodigy in a country that pushed its young sporting stars almost to breaking point, Shevchenko was on the traditional path that all young Soviet footballers followed. He played in the junior ranks of the state Red Army team, Dynamo Kiev, and then graduated into the first team before the soccer scouts from the West started to turn their attentions to the newly accessible Eastern-bloc teams. He came to prominence, ironically, in the 1998–99 Champions League, the season that United won the trophy. He

scored eight Champions League goals for Kiev as they battled through to the semi-finals, where they were only narrowly beaten by Bayern Munich. The Germans then, of course, met United in the final in Barcelona, losing out to Solskjaer and Sheringham in added-on time. By the start of the next season, Shevchenko had moved to AC Milan where, in 2003, he and his team-mates won the Champions League final after a penalty shoot-out against Juventus at, of all places, Old Trafford.

RUUD VAN NISTELROOY

Wayne Rooney knows more about Ruud van Nistelrooy than any other player in the world. They are, of course, United's first-choice strike-force and have to be able to read each other's minds to be as effective as they can be. And the Dutchman who will lead his country's strike force in the World Cup is one of the all-time scoring stars of the Champions League. By the end of the 2005–06 competition he had scored forty-one goals and

Rooney has no hesitation in classifying him as one of the world's great marksmen. He said, 'He's in a class of his own. I'm glad I don't have to play in teams against him very often, because I know how much damage he can do. He scores goals in the area, whereas I get some of mine from further out. If I was a defender I would be having nightmares, because you never know where he's suddenly going to pop up.'

The admiration is not all one-way traffic though. Van Nistelrooy has said, 'Wayne is one of the best young players in the world and he has a huge future. It's fantastic to play alongside him. I have been blown away by his performances since he arrived at the club. Most players find their first year at a new club quite hard, but Wayne didn't have any problems.

'You don't normally see people of that age with his

kind of ability. He is strong, can take people on and is able to play in so many different positions. He has played up front, on the left and the right, in midfield and in the hole.'

These are the four top men who Rooney believes will make the biggest impact on the competition up-front, with particular relevance to England's progress. Indeed, England could meet van Nistelrooy's Holland as early as the second round of the competition. Let's assume that England win their group, B, and that Holland finish second to Argentina in group C, ahead of Serbia and the Ivory Coast. If that happens, then England and Holland will play each other in the second round.

Ronaldo's Brazil could well meet England in the semi-finals of the competition, while there seems little danger that Shevchenko's Ukraine and Henry's France will not go forward from their groups, given the fact that they have to deal with countries as feeble as Saudi Arabia and Togo along the way.

In addition to these established world-class stars, there will also be a host of young upstarts trying to use the stage in Germany to launch themselves into the world spotlight.

LIONEL MESSI

The youngest and most outstanding player in the world next to Rooney is generally recognised as Argentina's Lionel Messi. At just eighteen years of age, he has the same sort of advanced footballer's mind and developed body as Rooney. He has been tagged 'Little Bull' because of his tremendous physique: his neck is the same width as his head; his thighs are like those of a rider in the Tour de France; and he has the ability to make other players bounce off him. He also exhibits the same ruthless self-belief, determination and fiery temperament of The Roon.

Although he is destined to become the biggest Argentinian star since Maradona, he has not lived in his native country since he was thirteen years old. His family's forefathers are Spanish and, when he was just thirteen, his parents decided to relocate to Europe.

By that stage, his outstanding talent had already become obvious, but he was plagued by a hormone deficiency that couldn't be successfully treated by doctors at home. With the prospect of a future football career becoming hampered, it was decided that he had a better chance of recovery in Spain – a country with established football links with Argentina. He joined Barcelona juniors as soon as he arrived in Spain and averaged a goal per game throughout his junior years.

Like Rooney, he announced his arrival on the first-team stage at his club with a spectacular goal. He came on as substitute to try and revive the game against Albacete and, within a minute of replacing Samuel Eto'o, he chipped in a wonder goal from the edge of the area.

This season, 2005–06, he has been so outstanding for Barcelona alongside Ronaldinho that his new five-year contract contains a clause that would compensate the club to the tune of an astonishing £100 million if any other club in the world to tried to buy him out of it.

Barcelona manager Frank Rijkaard said, 'He is very, very special. It's hard to believe sometimes that he is so young, because he has gained the respect of the other players and has become a crucial part of the team ... There is no limit to what he can achieve. The World Cup will not frighten him at all and he will be better for it. The bigger the competition, the more he likes it. He will come back to us as an even better player.'

However, Messi's international debut was not as successful as Rooney's. He was sent off after just ninety seconds of the game against Hungary, but such is the adulation that already surrounds him, he was instantly forgiven and is quickly becoming the favourite in an Argentinian team loaded with stars.

CRISTIANO RONALDO

Rooney's team-mate Cristiano Ronaldo is bound to be touted as one of the youngsters who will flourish during the World Cup. Though his country, Portugal, are not one of the strongest teams on show in Germany, he will still almost certainly get a long run in the competition, as they are in one of the easiest groups, D, along with Angola, Iran and Mexico.

Ronaldo is more like a South American player than a European one. He is the master of the step-over, very much in the style of the Brazilian wonder boy Robinho, but as a result, he has been accused more than once of being a 'show-pony'.

It has even brought protests from his team-mates, because while his style of football is highly entertaining, it can also be frustratingly inconsistent. If a spectacular jinking move down the wing results in a goal, or sets up a strike, then all is well. But all too often he can run into trouble and seems reluctant to accept that football can be played just as effectively in a more simple fashion.

According to reports, he was subjected to anger and criticism from his team-mates after United crashed out of the Champions League at Benfica in December 2005. Ryan Giggs was substituted, but was alleged to have said, 'What about him?' while pointing at Ronaldo.

Other members of the team had a go at the Portuguese player, accusing him of playing up to his homeland crowd with step-overs and even juggling tricks. And later, the club coach Carlos Querioz, also Portuguese, admitted, 'All of us agree that he did not have one of his best performances.'

But with his undoubted talent, he has the ability to tear a full-back apart all afternoon with a burst of speed, a dropped shoulder and a mesmerising run to the line.

With van Nistelrooy and Louis Saha waiting in the middle, and with Rooney lurking on the edge of the area, there is always going to be somebody waiting to put to use a fast and curling cross from either side.

Ronaldo joined United as a virtual unknown from Sporting Lisbon in 2003, when he was still only eighteen years of age. He had been with them for six years, but had never really got himself noticed until in his last year.

The late, great George Best, perhaps the greatest British footballer to date, in trademark mesmerising action in 1970.

Even then it was almost by mistake that he joined United. The two clubs played a pre-season friendly and very soon afterwards he was transferred to Old Trafford.

His finest hour in a red shirt came in the 2004 FA Cup final when he put in an outstanding performance, including a goal, during Manchester United's 3-0 win over Millwall.

His individual skills will undoubtedly light up the World Cup, but the question mark will remain as to whether or not he has the overall impact on a game to lift his national team in the way that Rooney would be expected to lift England and Messi the Argentinians.

One thing you cannot take away from him, however, is a rare accolade that came from George Best. The Manchester United legend said of him, 'There have been a few players described as "the new George Best", but this is the first time that I have ever regarded it as a compliment.'

CESC FABREGAS

A late contender who could emerge from Germany 06 as the greatest young player in the world is the eighteen-year-old Arsenal sensation, Cesc Fabregas.

The Spanish youth is yet another product of the talent spotting genius of the Gunner's manager, Arsène Wenger. Fabregas caught the attention of the world when Arsenal played Juventus at Highbury in their Champion's League campaign.

It was forecast that he would be buried in midfield by the former Arsenal skipper and driving force, Patrick Vieira, who had moved to the Italian champions the previous summer.

But showing an astonishing maturity, Fabregas, already a Spanish international, took a total grip of the game, dominated the midfield, scored one goal and made the other in a 2-0 victory.

He had long been touted as the boy who could replace Vieira but had not really established himself as completely as the fans would have liked until the Champions League tie.

Afterwards he was hailed as a phenomenon. Newspaper headline screamed 'Absolutely Fabregas' and 'Worldbeater Cesc'.

Significantly he was referred to as London's answer to Wayne Rooney.

But to put it into perspective he was only receiving the sort of acclaim that the Croxteth Kid enjoyed when he scored his first astonishing senior goal, ironically of course against Arsenal.

The World Cup in Germany represents the first big international tournament for the Arsenal youngster but the second opportunity for Rooney.

And the Spaniard will not be playing in an international team that is anything like as strong as England. Spain are serial disappointers in international competitions.

The Catalan whizz-kid grew up in a family devoted to FC Barcelona. He first watched a game there as a nine-month old baby perched on his grand-father's knee.

His presence at Arsenal is special because he has exhibited the same sort of ambition to succeed – and bloody-mindedeness – as Rooney. Like Rooney his aim was to become a star of his home club. But when opportunities didn't come fast enough in the youth ranks he responded to Arsenal's invitation and left for England.

He started life in London living in digs and training morning and afternoon. At week-ends he flew home to be with his family.

Also like his English opposite he has a devoted girlfriend. He has known Carla since she was 16.

Reflecting on his rise to fame, he said: 'I am really happy to have made the move from Barcelona to Arsenal when I was so young. I have to thank all the people who believe in me.

'I can't wait for the World Cup. Who doesn't want to be in the World Cup?'

EIGHT

THE FUTURE'S BRIGHT, THE FUTURE'S ROONEY

IN THE HISTORY of the beautiful game, only the legendary Pelé comes anywhere close to emulating the achievements of Wayne Rooney at such a young age. The boy from a humble terraced house on one of Britain's most downtrodden housing estates already sits at the peak of footballing history.

As a consequence, in his relentless march to immortality, Wayne Rooney seems certain to become the most capped player England has ever produced. He has set off at such a dynamic pace that he could achieve the milestone by the age of thirty-one – and still have up to four years after that to build up an unassailable figure of international caps.

By his twentieth birthday, The Roon had already racked up twenty-six international appearances. The target he is chasing is the 125 caps held by legendary England goalkeeper Peter Shilton.

179

Goalkeepers traditionally play on longer than outfield players, so Rooney's achievement will be all the greater; perhaps his most notable feat will come if he beats the 108 international appearances achieved by World Cup-winning captain Bobby Moore. On current projections – with England playing up to eleven games a season or more, depending on their progress in international competitions – he could well have achieved that feat by his twenty-ninth birthday.

Amazingly, Rooney already has the record of having played more games at his age than Pelé had done – twenty-six to twenty-three, although Pelé did manage twenty-five goals in those appearances, at an astonishing ratio of more than one per game.

'It's wonderful when you see a young player start to realise what he can achieve. He's precious.'

Pelé

On the subject of goals, that is the other target that the Croxteth Kid already has in his sights as he is set to become England's most prolific goalscorer: in his first twenty-six games for England, he has scored ten goals. On a ratio basis, that means he is well on the road to beating Bobby Charlton's total of forty-nine goals. One also has to bear in mind that, traditionally, players tend to be hesitant in the goal-scoring charts early in their careers and more prolific as they play more games.

If we look at the facts, Rooney already has a big start on the footballing knight, for Charlton had won not a single cap by the time he was twenty. The Manchester United legend is only one of a list of England's great players, both past and present, who had not even been called into an international squad by the age that Rooney was heading towards thirty full caps. Among the others are David Beckham, Paul Gascoigne and Gary Lineker. And that is not a phenomenon solely restricted to these shores; some of the most famous players of all time – including Zinedine Zidane, Roberto Baggio and England's tormentor in the 1970 World Cup, Gerd Muller – had neither won a cap nor scored a goal at the same stage of their life.

'He's going to get better, which is frightening.'
David Beckham

Rooney is the most iconic footballer we have had in this country since Paul Gascoigne, who was as much a product of the Geordie culture as Rooney is of the Scouse, and who was hailed as the genius of his age and the greatest talent this country had produced since the World Cup-winning days of the 1960s.

However, if you compare the records of the two sorcerers, it becomes clear that Rooney is light-years ahead of his north-eastern counterpart: it is something that places the young Merseysider's achievements truly into perspective.

Gascoigne had to wait until his twenty-sixth birthday before he reached the same stage that Rooney had achieved by the age of twenty. In fact, the most outstanding British talent to come anywhere near to

Gazza in his prime at World Cup Italia '90.

Rooney's achievements at the same age is Norman Whiteside – who represented Northern Ireland in the 1982 World Cup when he was seventeen and who had gained twenty-one caps by the time he was twenty. He had also scored seven goals by then.

Norman Whiteside, aged 17, warms up against Spain in 1982.

Michael Owen had won sixteen caps and scored five goals at the same age, while Duncan Edwards, the Manchester United prodigy who lost his life in the Munich air crash, had won nine caps and scored one goal.

The Merseyside phenomenon's unique pace of achievement in youth is not restricted to British comparisons. Ronaldo and Marco van Basten are also way behind him in the age profiles: even Maradona lags behind.

The coach who guided Rooney through his formative years, former Everton manager and star footballer himself Colin Harvey, has no doubts about how far Rooney can go. He said, 'He can become one of the greatest players English football has ever seen. It's a hell of a tall order, but he's got all the attributes. As well as his strength, he's got pace, he's good in the air and he's a tremendous athlete. He's two-footed and although he is weaker on his left side, he will work on that.

'He was England's player of the tournament in 2004, but that didn't surprise me at all because I always knew what he could do. He could become as good as Maradona. Even better. I think he's the best talent since

Maradona and I've always rated the Argentinian a better all-round performer than Pelé.'

The table below illustrates Rooney's achievements against an international array of all-time greats.

HOW ROONEY'S ACHIEVEMENTS AT AGE 20 COMPARE:		
PLAYER	CAPS	GOALS
Wayne Rooney (England)	26	10
Pelé (Brazil)	23	25
Norman Whiteside (Northern Ireland)	21	7
Diego Maradona (Argentina)	20	8
Robbie Keane (Ireland)	18	6
Gheorghe Hagi (Romania)	16	2
Michael Owen (England)	16	5
Ronaldinho (Brazil)	14	8
Ronaldo (Brazil)	13	5
Cristiano Ronaldo (Portugal)	11	5
Patrick Kluivert (Holland)	10	4
Duncan Edwards (England)	9	1
Raúl (Spain)	7	1
Paolo Maldini (Italy)	7	0
Gianni Rivera (Italy)	6	2
Dennis Law (Scotland)	6	1
Fernando Torres (Spain)	6	1
Diego Simeone (Argentina)	6	0
Marco van Basten (Holland)	4	2
Rio Ferdinand (England)	4	0
Johan Cruyff (Holland)	2	1
Stanley Matthews (England)	2	1
Franz Beckenbauer (Germany)	2	0
Lother Matthaus (Germany)	1	0

ZERO CAPS BY AGE 20:
David Beckham
Jermain Defoe
Steven Gerrard
Frank Lampard
Alan Shearer
Glenn Hoddle
Paul Gascoigne
Bobby Charlton
Bobby Moore
Gary Lineker
Francesco Totti
Thierry Henry
Zinedine Zidane
David Trezeguet
Ruud van Nistelrooy
Dennis Bergkamp
Jurgen Klinsmann
Gerd Muller
Gabriel Batistuta
Gianluca Vialli
Roberto Baggio
Jim Baxter
Pavel Nedved

Of course Rooney's future achievements depend on a number of factors:

INJURY

Rooney broke the metatarsal in his right foot during Euro 2004 when he had only just burst onto the international scene; and again, broke it only weeks before the World Cup in Germany 2006 – exactly the same injury that afflicted Michael Owen in the build-up. And he is in even better company as a metatarsal breaker: England colleagues David Beckham, Steven Gerrard and Gary Neville have all suffered the same fate.

Many believe that Rooney's injury cost England the tournament at Euro 2004; once he went off the field against Portugal in the quarter-finals, it was clear that England lost both their shape and the game. But apart from what could have been two more games in that competition, it did not cost Rooney in the long-term when it came to the international calendar. As yet it is not clear what the impact of his second metatarsal break will have on his immediate competitive achievements this year.

The injury can take varying amounts of time to heal, depending on the extent of the break and the individual concerned. In Rooney's case it was fourteen weeks before he was fully fit to play again in 2004. In contrast, Newcastle's Scott Parker was frustrated for nearly a year as complications set in with his recovery.

It is a sad fact that some players are naturally injury-prone and have to battle throughout their careers to try and find a consistent run of games without the interruption of a knock, a strain or a tear.

The best example of this in modern times is Darren Anderton. Throughout his years at Tottenham, Anderton was constantly plagued with problems – to the extent where he became infamous to every football fan with the nickname 'Sick Note'.

Despite the latest setback, Rooney is generally considered to be an injury-free footballer in the same mould as Frank Lampard and John Terry. There are a few reasons for this: some physical and others more psychological.

The first one was described to me by a Pemiership professional, who is still playing and who, therefore, must remain nameless. He said, 'When you are lined up in the tunnel and you look across at the other team you try to avoid Rooney's eyes. He looks like he wants to kill you. He snorts like a bull with his chest heaving in and out and sometimes he turns his back and starts kicking the wall with his boots. You feel sorry for the wall. I've even seen him punching the wall.

'The effect of seeing his name written on the back of his shirt is also unsettling, because he's made such fools of so many defenders that you just fear from that moment on that you are going to have a dreadful day.

'Then, just before the ref leads us out, he starts shouting, really bellowing, at his team-mates, most of whom are much older than him. He clearly can't wait to get going. You get the feeling that if the ref delayed us for just another few seconds there would be an earthquake in that tunnel.'

Rooney is regarded, even among his peers, as a 'hard' footballer. That doesn't mean that he goes around clobbering people, but that when players tackle him they have described it as like hitting a lamppost in a darkened street.

He has tremendous body strength. He comes from a family of boxers and, according to his boys' club coaches, could easily have become a pugilist. This manifests itself in the phenomenon of players bouncing off him when they are challenging him for the ball.

Wayne never shies from 50-50 balls. Here he shows commitment to challenging Sorin in the victory over Argentina in November 2005.

Once professionals have become aware of the fact that Rooney seems to have a protective shield around him, they are reluctant to go in again because they fear that they will find themselves winded or flat on their face and, therefore, not much use to their team-mates.

Another factor that usually keeps him injury-free is his dynamic speed and his ability to avoid, evade and jump free from potential aggressors. George Best had exactly the same talent to keep out of physical trouble.

It is astonishing that in ten years of top-flight football, Best was hardly ever injured. And that was in the days when referees were nowhere near as protective of players as they are today: tackling from behind was allowed; players didn't have to wear shin-pads and if you ever went to a game in which Best was playing, you would often hear the opposition coaches shouting, 'Break the bastard's legs!'

Referees have learned over the years to be particular aware of 'roughhouse' tactics against our better players, but nevertheless it is still a testament to the guile of the Merseysider that it is so difficult to clock him.

Paul Gascoigne is a tragic example of a player who lost a huge amount of his career through injury. Amazingly, Gazza was only ever available for selection for half of the games in which he could have played. This constituted a real waste of talent.

CLUBS AND MANAGERS

So far, Wayne has had successful spells at two great English clubs. Everton brought him into the game from the age of nine and it was in a blue shirt that he exploded onto both the Premiership and then the world stage. To many he will remain an Evertonian forever. But, as he has explained, circumstances conspired to take him away from Everton and on to Manchester United. He felt it was right at the time and he has since pledged his entire future to the world's biggest club.

It's clear that he thrives on the biggest stages and United usually recognised as being the biggest club in the world. Rooney has gone on the record to say that he wants to spend his entire career with the club, and although that is a noble ambition at twenty years of age, it is impossible to see what the future is going to bring.

Rooney's first manager as a professional was David Moyes, a strict disciplinarian who had had an average career as a footballer but who has now carved out an outstanding role as a team boss. At the end of the

Rooney merchandise outside the biggest club in the world, his image held in the same commercial regard as the legendary Man Utd player of yesteryear, George Best.

2004–05 season, he was voted the manager of the year by his fellow managers.

Wayne had a lively relationship with the steely-eyed Moyes. Here was a young man of exceptional talent who would have played five times a week if he could have done. And in charge of him was a young manager who was handed the delicious problem of nurturing the greatest English talent to emerge in the game for decades.

David Moyes was often criticised for holding Wayne back. Instead of starting games, the prodigy often found himself on the bench and even if he did start, he was often hauled off in the second half. Rooney demonstrated his frustration and anger at being substituted on more than one occasion.

At international level his career seemed to be bounding ahead, but at club level Moyes erred on the side of caution. Some believed that by sending Rooney on at a later stage of the game, particularly when Everton might have been losing, added even more pressure onto his still-developing shoulders.

It was as if he was being taken off the leash and told to get on there and win it for Everton. The player himself never felt as though it was pressure; he just wanted to play and if in the process he could help Everton to win a game, then that was a dream come true for a boy who still bristled with pride every time he walked down the tunnel at Goodison Park and heard the *Z Cars* theme music blaring out.

Moyes has always defended his strategy with Rooney and he markedly points out that Rooney is now rated as one of the best – indeed, he now carries the title of World Young Player of the Year.

For months after Rooney burst on to the scene by scoring the goal against Arsenal in October 2002, the manager kept his counsel on his protégé. Even after Wayne made his debut as England's youngest ever player in February of the following year, Moyes did not want to raise the temperature and heap more pressure on the boy.

The lad was getting rave reviews at international level and that again was fuelling the calls, mostly in Liverpool, that Rooney should start every game. There were even some suggestions that the club manager wasn't overly pleased that his player had become a regular fixture in the international set-up. Talking ahead of England's home game against Turkey in the European Championship qualifiers in May 2003 at Sunderland, Moyes rebuked these ideas, saying, 'Everton will have a team that will be good enough to give Wayne Rooney the platform that a talent like his deserves. He is such a natural. Even at this age he has the ability to do most things asked of him. I've warned people not to expect too much too soon of him and that's been regarded as a criticism of Sven-Goran Eriksson for picking him. But I was absolutely delighted when he called up Wayne. There's no problem with me that he is in the spotlight.'

Rooney went on to play in that game and was rated as Man of the Match in England's winning performance. His club manager was full of praise, but he still had a fatherly word or two of caution.

He said, 'He is capable of these performances and they will become more regular as he gets stronger and fitter. That's what we have to aim for, but we have to be careful. Hopefully he has loads and loads of games to come for Everton and loads more caps to come for England. And if we think that, he doesn't need to be pushed today.

'I have to do what is right for Everton and, more importantly what is right for Wayne Rooney. If you look at Wayne's performances, he did better as a substitute than he did in the games he started. He made a big impact when he came on and out of those he started, he was very good – excellent in a few of them. Remember, he was a boy who had just come out of school. He'd had no full-time training.'

Further public support for the eighteen-year-old came in December 2003. Moyes did not know then that Rooney was to leave the club by the early weeks of the following season as a legend. But as that legend was continuing to build, the Premiership's youngest manager said, 'He is a young boy who is doing terrifically well. We are very pleased with him. He is a special talent who is only eighteen and we are trying to nurture that talent and bring him on as much as we possibly can.'

Since Rooney changed clubs, the two men have maintained a good relationship. These days, before a fixture between the two clubs, you will invariably find them chatting with each other in a quiet corner of the stadium.

When he moved to Manchester United, he came under the control of Sir Alex Ferguson. The greatest young talent in the game was suddenly under the aegis of the most successful manager of the day – and a man with a fearsome reputation as a harsh disciplinarian.

Right from the start, Ferguson seemed to be in awe of his new signing. He said later that he had been after him since he was sixteen and that United had even offered £5 million in those days, before Rooney had even hit football's radar screen.

On the day that Rooney turned up at Old Trafford and signed for Manchester United, Ferguson assumed a benevolent, fatherly smile, one that continues to light up his face whenever he talks about the player.

Rooney with new manager Ferguson, plus Coleen and agent Paul Stretford, on his day of signing for Manchester United, and below, one lucky local fan meets his new idol.

Managers at all levels of the game are usually loath to single out any one member of their squad for praise. But Ferguson has no such qualms about Rooney – neither for that matter do his other coaches at Old Trafford and even his team-mates and club captain.

Ferguson had not the slightest hesitation in shelling out a world record fee for an eighteen-year-old – a fee that could total nearly £30 million.

And Rooney repaid his faith with one of the greatest debuts ever witnessed in modern-day football. He scored the perfect hat-trick in the Champions League tie against Fenerbahce at Old Trafford, one with his left foot, one with the right and then an unbeatable free-kick.

Ferguson battled with himself to try and play the situation down, because he knew the dangers of young players receiving too much praise too early in their career. Nevertheless, it prompted the United boss to say, 'It's a great start for him. That's why we signed him. He's got great potential ... I think he can only get stronger. The important thing for me as a coach is to allow the boy to develop naturally without too much public attention. I want him to be as ordinary as he can.'

> **The boy wonder seemed to feel no pressure as he scored a hat-trick on his Manchester United debut in the Champions League against Turkish club Fenerbahce. Following the phenomenal performance, he was named the PFA Fans' Player of the Month for October 2004.**

In the run-up to the World Cup, Rooney was hitting top form and being nominated as Man of the Match game after game. His profile came into even greater focus as news emerged that Manchester United legend George Best was losing his battle for life.

United's first game after Best's death was against West Ham. Rooney had said in tribute to Best that he hopes he is remembered in much the same way. He then produced another ten-out-of-ten performance, scoring a stunning goal as United came from behind to win 2-1.

Ferguson said, 'I hoped that somebody would produce moments that would reflect George Best properly ... Wayne is only twenty and without question is the best young player that I have seen in my time. If he keeps developing and matures, goodness knows what he will become. He's a breath of fresh air to the game. He could have scored four or five today. He produced some great moments.'

Though few people have ever considered Rooney as a leader of men, probably because he is still so very young, Sir Alex sees qualities in the boy that he thinks could make him a club captain of the future.

He said, 'I think we have a potential captain in Wayne Rooney. I think there are indications there that he has the mental toughness, respect and the winning mentality that Manchester United captains need.'

Ferguson clearly sees Rooney as a boy made in his own image – and in the image of the former captain Roy Keane, who moved on to Celtic after a blast too many at his team-mates for performing badly in a match they lost.

The Manchester United manager is taken by Rooney's focus and desire, explaining, 'He's a product of being brought up just thinking about football. There are many examples of that – Roy Keane, Bryan Robson, Mark Hughes – who combine that great energy and passion to play football all the time. It doesn't matter the kind of game; you get the same desire and commitment every time. It's refreshing to see someone so young have that.'

'He never seems to feel the pressure of the big games. His abilities are there for everyone to see. He's an outstanding young player and hopefully he will improve even more.'

Former Man Utd captain Roy Keane

Nobody knows how long Rooney will stay at Manchester United. That depends on the individual views of both the player and the club and it is very rare these days for a footballer to spend nearly his whole career at one club.

Rooney may have pledged himself to United for life, but so much can happen over the next few years. His principal motivation for playing football is to win things.

He says, 'My ambitions in a Manchester United shirt are quite simple. A club this size should be winning trophies and I think we have a good enough squad to be doing exactly that.

'At this club we want to win every tournament we are in. First of all we want the league, but of course the Champions League is massive for us as well. The number of trophies won here in the past is frightening – the current set of lads want to add to that great history.'

Nobody doubts Rooney's commitment to his club, but things change very quickly at the top of the football tree and Rooney joined Manchester United just as they were coming down from the crest of a decade-long wave of astonishing success.

Ferguson no doubt believed that Rooney's arrival would revive the club's pursuit of excellence, but too many other faults started to appear in the fabric of the team that had conquered the world.

Beckham, inspirational to his team-mates and an icon of football in this country had gone. Roy Keane, the Panzer-tank-like captain was struggling to play full seasons through wear and tear, and a succession of new midfield players to form the next generation had not come up to scratch.

Firepower up front was lacking. In previous seasons, the club had had four class forwards to choose from. But when Rooney arrived, there was nobody apart from the brilliant Ruud van Nistelrooy.

At the same time, the 'Chelski' revolution at Stamford Bridge was in full swing. Russian billionaire Roman Abramovich was pumping hundreds of millions of pounds into the club and the result was their first title in fifty years in the first season that Rooney played for United.

Chelsea's domination could last for years. They have almost limitless amounts of money and billionaire Mr Abramovich seems to have quelled any fears that his interest in Chelsea was going to be a passing fancy with the club now openly talking about spending another few hundred million on a new ground.

So where does this leave Wayne Rooney ?

He loves the 'bigness' of the set-up at Old Trafford and truly believes he is playing for the top club in the world. There is no question that his heart has been stolen by

© By John Ingledew

Roman Abramovich celebrates winning the 2005 Premiership with John Terry, Frank Lampard and Eidur Gudjohnsen.

United and he has already pledged himself to them for the long term.

Nevertheless, there is not a more ambitious player in this country. He went through tremendous soul-searching when he left Everton, a club that was branded into his soul. And he did it because of his ambition to compete, and more importantly to win, at the top. At his age he has plenty of time to achieve his ambitions in the north-west of England.

He has joined United during one of their transition periods. Other players, like Dwight Yorke and Andy Cole, joined them during a decade of dominance and duly have the medals to prove the contributions they made to that continuing success.

At his age, Rooney has plenty of time to emulate those achievements, but he is restless for glory and he will almost certainly inherit a new boss in the next couple of years. United could find themselves in the position that they will soon be under pressure to produce ten other players worthy of Rooney's presence.

At Portugal 2004, the then-fledgling striker looked on in admiration at the records of the Manchester United players in the dressing room. Today, his eyes turn enviously towards the Chelsea and Liverpool players. I don't think he has any ambitions to join either of those two clubs, but he wants to be a recognised winner. He will pursue that ambition in a ruthless fighting fashion both on and off the field.

There is also the possibility that he could become bigger than the club itself. He is set to become the most valuable footballer in the world. Look at what has happened to former players in that position. Their currency is so high that they become immensely valuable to a club as a marketable asset. What club, for instance, would have let Maradona go at his peak? None, you would have thought, but he changed hands several times, even though he was the best player in the world.

Similarly, why would a gigantic club like Barcelona let the world's top player, Ronaldo, move on? It's because of the way that football works these days. Money is the most potent force in the game.

And the player is only one element that benefits financially in a big transfer deal. Sometimes he is powerless to stop a transfer, because circumstances whirling above his head result in him moving on.

OFF-FIELD ACTIVITIES

Rooney also has to keep himself fit off the field. He lives

in a world where he has been a millionaire since he was eighteen. For a lad from a humble home, that brings terrible temptations.

Among his generation, Rooney is not regarded as either a boozer or a club-lover. Unlike others who have fallen by the wayside, he has been in a stable relationship for all of his short, yet dynamic, professional life to date. But the pitfalls are everywhere.

There are two outstanding examples of professional footballers who torpedoed the latter parts of their careers through abuse off the field.

The most spectacular case in point is that of George Best, who died in late 2005 after decades of heavy, and often riotous, boozing.

But Best was not what you would describe as a 'sad' character. By the time he gave up playing football at the highest level he was only twenty-seven, but he had won big honours in the game, including the European Cup.

The Belfast Boy enjoyed his boozing years tremendously and once confessed to Jimmy Greaves – a soccer legend who has stood firm against alcoholism for nearly thirty years – that if he could have done a deal with God to drink happily for five more years and then die, he would have taken it.

The second example is that of Paul Gascoigne. Gascoigne has been, and remains, a far more complicated character than Best. The former England player has a self-declared drink problem, one that, at one time, could see him swigging the entire contents of a bottle of whisky in twenty minutes. In addition, he has a highly compulsive nature that he battles to control. It manifests itself in repetitive actions, such as opening and closing his front door over and over again until he is happy that he has closed it properly. Or he may leave his house and get five miles away before deciding to go back, afraid he has not arranged the towels properly in his bathroom.

Gascoigne's mental fragility was first displayed in the 1991 FA Cup final as he lined up with his Tottenham Hotspur team to take on Brian Clough's Nottingham Forest. First, he shattered royal protocol when he took the hand of Diana, Princess of Wales, and kissed it. Then, when the teams broke to warm up before the kick-off, it was obvious that Gazza was hyper. Instead of stretching and sprinting or passing the ball around, he decided to go in goal and started shouting at the other players to fire balls at him.

Early in the game, he clattered into Forest's Gary Charles and came off worse; it resulted in him being carried off on a stretcher with cruciate ligament damage to the knee – an injury that in those days was very likely to end a player's career.

He spent a year recuperating in this country while his new bosses from the Italian club Lazio, who had paid £5 million for him before the FA Cup final, looked on nervously to see if he would ever recover properly.

The Geordie hero didn't help himself by returning to his native North-East during his convalescence and getting himself involved in a mysterious incident in a night-club in which he ended up sprawled on the floor in the men's loo with his knee having suffered another knock.

He eventually returned to full-time football and, although nothing spectacular happened for him in Italy, he went to Rangers in Scotland and had many more years in the game until his largely unspectacular career petered out.

But he was blighted by injuries. And the worst part of his breaks, tears and pulls was the length of time it took for them to clear up. One doctor came up with the theory that he was a slow healer because there was insufficient oxygen in his blood.

What he really meant was that Gazza used to drink so much that his veins were overloaded with alcohol, pushing oxygen out and delaying the healing process. Oxygen carried in the blood is essential when it comes to helping a bone, a muscle or a ligament to get better. Take David Beckham, for instance: he spent hours sitting in an oxygen tank when he broke his foot before the 2002 World Cup to try and speed up the knitting together of the bone. Wayne Rooney has now also found himself a resident of the oxygen tank in his battle against a broken metatarsal.

Those who know Rooney are aware of his single-mindedness and his terrific strength of character. He doesn't tolerate hangers-on or those who want to bask in his reflected glory. Unlike Gascoigne, he is unlikely to want to be pictured in the company of celebrity radio DJs and entertainers who might want to take advantage of the publicity value of their new friend.

In addition, he has a very solid relationship with girlfriend Coleen. So he is unlikely to be drawn into a life of debauchery unless he wants to be. And there is no evidence of that so far.

In fact, his desire to be his own man has been obvious from the very first time he was drafted into the senior England squad. One other young player appointed himself as Rooney's 'minder'. There was tremendous public interest in the then-Everton player, but each time a TV camera homed in on him, the other player suddenly appeared trying to put a protective arm around him.

After two days of this, Rooney felt that he could stand on his own two feet without any problem. He thanked his team-mate for the concern, but decided that if he was going to have to suffer being under the spotlight throughout his career, then he may as well get used to it. He'd handled himself okay on the streets of Croxteth for the past seventeen years, so he had no fears.

DESIRE VS REWARDS

Wayne Rooney is on course to become the first ever billion-dollar footballer. When you think that agents representing David Beckham are already working on image-rights equations that they say value their player at £300,000 a week, it is easy to see how the money could add up over a possible fifteen-year career.

> Rooney now holds an account at Coutts, the posh bank where the Queen keeps her money.

Footballers can retire these days with endorsement contracts for the next thirty years and when you look at how the world gets richer every day, it's not beyond the realms of possibility to consider the phenomenon of a billon-dollar footballer.

As the appeal of the game continues to grow around the world, with ever-expanding TV networks and communications, the Croxteth Kid is set to become a global icon. His wealth would be measured in US dollars, the currency that will be used between massive developing economies like India and China, and the Western deal-makers.

> Rooney has been adopted by the Chinese as their number-one pin-up – and nicknamed 'Baby Elephant' because of his mixture of 'charm, tantrums and occasional clumsiness'! Closer to home, he has been dubbed 'The Baby Bomber' in Italy and 'The Messiah' in Spain.

The richest sportsman in the world is currently the golfer Tiger Woods. His likely billionaire status before he retires is already accepted among sporting marketeers.

Golf as a sport has had at least a three-decade headstart on football in terms of capitalising on the appeal value of the game to both audiences and sponsors. It has grabbed and retained the more sophisticated area of sponsorship. Designer clothes labels, watch and jewellery manufacturers and producers of the more refined range of drinks are all anxious to climb on board. Historically, this contrasts with football, which is still regarded as the 'working-man's game' around the world.

Though corporate sponsorship is attracting many more people from the higher socio-economic areas, it is still fundamentally the 'people's game'.

Whereas in the past this positioning of the sport has had a negative effect on revenue-earning potential, conversely it will soon be the catalyst for a huge expansion of income in the future.

Rooney has swooped on a host of sponsorship deals to boost his personal wealth: Asda, £3m; Nike, £5m, Coca-Cola, £1m; and a £3m deal with Electronic Arts, which produces the computer game Fifa '06 starring Rooney and Ronaldinho, the Brazil and Barcelona star.

When every working person in China and India has a television in every room of their house, they may well be in a position to want to consume around-the-clock football.

European football and, in many cases, the English Premiership, is still the most popular in the world. Look what could happen in the future.

There are a billion people in China. If just one percent of the population were to pay US$1 to watch a pay-per-view game, that would raise $10 million per game.

If, by then, Manchester United, for example, owned their own TV rights through MUTV, that would give them $380 million (about £200 million) a season from their home games for TV rights in China alone.

When you think of India and the football-mad Far Eastern countries like Thailand and Singapore, the figures become incalculable.

And, as has always been the case, the greatest percentage of a club's income goes on players' salaries. And the best players get the most money.

Weekly salaries for players of up to £300,000 are already being talked about. David Beckham's advisers are studying sums relating to the image rights benefits to his club, which they believe could reach those sort of figures and these astronomical numbers do not even include the personal sponsorship deals.

Rooney already has a host of contracts with drinks companies, electronic games manufacturers, boot suppliers, clothing labels and even supermarkets. Even at the age of twenty, the England youngster is estimated to be worth at least £20 million on current and projected earnings.

That figure could double each year of his professional life and, if he becomes the best footballer in the world

and wins World Cups, it becomes almost impossible to calculate his future wealth.

Coleen is also contributing to the building of the cash mountain by herself securing deals worth £5 million for television and magazine work, promoting fashion and accessory labels and jointly promoting big-brand names with Wayne.

> **A talent agency scouring the country for Rooney look-alikes to take part in a new TV show had a few problems. London-based firm Juliet Adams said 'people who look like David Beckham are happier to go into the modelling business, but men who look like Wayne Rooney tend not to be such poseurs.'**

It has been said that Rooney does not have the 'pretty-boy' profile of David Beckham, who himself is thought to be heading for a retirement fortune of more than £100 million. But, in contrast, Beckham does not have the 'cheeky-little-kid' appeal that endears Rooney to youngsters who often then pester their parents to buy something endorsed by their hero.

> **Wayne's fortune has more than trebled to at least £20m in the past year. He and his fiancée, Coleen McLoughlin, have risen almost 50 places in the list of Britain's 100 wealthiest young people, published as part of the *Sunday Times Rich List 2006*.**

Rooney has a long-standing endorsement deal with Nike; here he is in February 2006 promoting their 'Joga Bonita' ('play beautiful') movement.

One renowned expert on football finance believes that the idea of Rooney achieving billion-dollar status is therefore completely viable.

Tom Cannon, Professor of Business at the University of Kingston, said, 'Not long ago, the suggestion that Wayne Rooney could be football's first billion-dollar man would have been greeted with derision. Now, as we see the wealth of today's richest football stars, the question becomes more real. David Beckham is worth at least $100 million and with good management will double that over the next few years.

'Rooney can be a far greater player. He remains England's best hope of winning the World Cup in Germany. Success could make him a national hero with massive earning potential. But Rooney is young enough to see England through two, three or four World Cups. Each success could be worth up to $50 million – on top of his normal career earnings of between $50–100 million. Add in the possibility of a major transfer or two and he is already there.

'You have to ask whether or not he has the looks, presence and support to become a Beckham-type global icon? Becks appeals to a specific audience, but it is all about positioning and, with the right presentation, Wayne could reach an equally valuable global marketplace.

'The sculpted body and ability to communicate –

which is getting notably better by the day – will take time. But the rewards are simply immense. Wayne can acquire these if he and his advisors – who seem to be on top of their game – spend the time and invest their resources.'

Every young professional footballer obviously has a desire for the game. It is often their ticket to escape from an average upbringing. Success in the game can, by comparison, give them entry to a world of riches and fame. But if that is their only motivation it is not enough.

Rooney has entered this world of wealth and privilege at a very young age. Is this a good thing or a bad thing?

Good thing: he got there very early and it's the only life he has ever known as an adolescent, so he will be desperate not to let it go. Or bad thing: because by his mid-twenties he may take it all for granted and could become bored with both his life and with football.

When a footballer loses his desire to play, everything else collapses. When footballers are as young as Rooney, there is little harm in going out on the lash occasionally. Physically it doesn't really matter; whatever damage they do at that age can be restored in one training session.

The problem in modern-day football usually comes mid-career. A good footballer can earn about £40,000 a week. Over a three-year contract that is £6 million. If a player aged twenty-five in that position wakes up one morning to find he has lost his automatic place, he has two choices: either fight to get back into the first team or roll over and count the dosh.

Few players have actually given the game up, but many have drifted into a different approach to their job with the cushion of wealth that is beyond the imagination of the vast majority of the population.

Eric Cantona is regarded as the most popular player ever to wear the Manchester United shirt. Over the next few years, Wayne Rooney will be competing for that title, but the iconic Frenchman has a huge regard for the young Englishman, yet warns of the pitfalls. He said, 'Manchester United are strong and always have the same kind of creative football. I love Rooney as a player. However, he is such a special talent that I sometimes worry. He can become the best player in the world at twenty-five if he knows that, in football, you have to be strong, train hard, go to bed early, be careful what you are eating and what you are drinking and what you do in life. If he still realises that at twenty-five, then he will be in the best three players in the world for many years. All the best players in the world know this. You cannot be a real player without being a great trainer. Practise, practise, practise.'

You can't define desire in a footballer or spot the moment when it starts to dissipate, but a manager and a player's team-mates can pick up on it as soon as it starts to happen.

Desire is also something that can take hold both on and off the pitch. Looking back again at Paul Gascoigne's career, it was always said that he would find life very difficult without football because of the turmoil in which he lived.

But if that is the case, then he understood less about his own life and his body than we may have realised. The extent of his drinking during his football career was so extensive that it is bound to have shortened his life as a professional footballer.

He was only ever fit to play in half the games that he could have been selected to play in and a lot of that was down to his slow healing process as already touched on.

Surely, if his desire for football was at the level it had been when he was running rings around kids on playing fields across Tyneside, then he might have taken more care of himself off the pitch to make sure that he was fit to play football.

Unfortunately, Gazza became a prime victim of an equation that works like this: young lad from working-class background becomes football superstar; that brings him untold riches, adulation and access to everything that anybody could want in life; as a result, he starts to live a lifestyle that although is a novelty at first, soon becomes normal and then becomes addictive. Net result: a loss of direction.

Who can say that that won't happen to Rooney?

Before turning 17 and becoming eligible for a professional contract Wayne was playing for £80 a week; he is now earning wages in excess of £50,000 a week, a figure which could be dwarfed in the near future.

Nobody at this stage. But one of the men who has shaped both his life and his career, Colin Harvey, believes that Rooney has the desire to be able to build a spectacular and long-lasting career.

He said, 'He has all the qualities to be a great, long-term England star. He's got all the attributes. Desire is at the top of them, alongside his ability. I know him and I know what he can do in the future.'

'There is nothing like scoring for your country – it's a great feeling. Scoring goals for your club is fantastic but, when it's England, the feeling is unbelievable.'

Wayne Rooney

Rooney's current desire and the inferno that burns within him which drives him to strive f or success at the World Cup is born out of his desperate need to want to win things.

When he was awarded the European Young Player of Europe award last year, he revealed, 'As far as I am aware, this is the first international trophy I have won. It's the only thing I have ever won since I was a kid. It's a nice feeling and I want a lot more of it.'

However, shortly afterwards, he experienced the pain of losing in the big arena and that was an experience he found so horrible that he never wants to go through it again.

Manchester United played Arsenal in the 2005 FA Cup final at the Millennium Stadium in Cardiff. United dominated the game and Rooney was arguably the Man of the Match, but his team lost on penalties.

Anybody who witnessed Rooney on the pitch after Arsenal had snatched the game could see that the hurt was distorting his face. Even though he could have comforted himself that he had years ahead of him to win trophies, it was no consolation.

As the Arsenal fans celebrated their victory over their fiercest rivals for the previous decade, Rooney stood in the middle of the boiling cauldron, hands on hips, with a look of total desolation on his face; a look that was slowly turning to a snarling, burning anger. Losing, as he described later, is the very worst feeling in the world.

Rooney has never had the slightest concern about the quality of the opposition or the surroundings in which he plays.

In his first game for Manchester United – the European tie with Fenerbahce – he scored a hat-trick, even though he'd never worn his new club's shirt before *and* it was his European debut. He said at the time that it wasn't any sense of fear that was going to inhibit his play that night, but the danger of getting over-excited.

The manager had told him he was playing two days beforehand and he couldn't contain his joy. He found it hard to sleep or to concentrate on anything except the upcoming game.

Anybody who has seen Rooney at close quarters will realise that he is unconcerned by his surroundings; he could be on his school playing field in Croxteth or in the Nou Camp – his desire remains the same.

After he scored the goal against Arsenal in 2002 that brought him to the world's attention as a sixteen-year-old prodigy, he gave the boots he wore that day to a Merseyside children's hospital. At the time, he was the youngest ever Premiership goalscorer, but he could not conceive the value of those boots in the future.

On one occasion, shortly after he had passed his driving test, he and Coleen were shopping in a hypermarket on the edge of Liverpool. They were out in Wayne's first ever car – a tiny Ford SportKa.

Wayne's fame as an Everton prodigy was in mid-

explosion. He might not have been as universally recognised as he is now, but this was Merseyside – his heartland.

The shopping had gone OK, as Wayne had dutifully pushed the trolley while Coleen filled it up with the pastas she was trying to wean him onto after a lifetime of a chips, sausages and beans diet.

Wayne had been wearing a baseball cap as he shopped, but had thrown it into the back seat. As they drove out of the hypermarket carpark, Wayne was forced to pull up sharply as his car and another converged at the exit.

> It cost a whopping £8,500 for Wayne to insure his first car. The number plate read 'ROO NI'!

He waved the other driver through: it was a lady driving a four-by-four. Wayne thought nothing off it and was puzzled when the other car didn't move as he gestured to let her go.

In fact, she was so shocked to see Rooney driving the car that she reached for her mobile phone to tell her husband, a keen Everton fan, that she had nearly driven into Wayne Rooney.

The woman was overcome with joy. She was blocking the exit, but was unaware of either the hooting of horns or the waving of arms. Wayne was stuck. If he had got out of the car to sort it out, it would have caused more commotion. He just had to wait until the star-struck woman came out of her trance.

Chaos ensued and it took a full fifteen minutes to clear the cars out of the way before he could reach the exit.

POSITION AND OPPORTUNITY

The next situation is where to play him. Indeed, it is not just international managers who struggle to find the perfect position for the boy – club managers have the same problem.

It is generally accepted that Rooney is outstanding in at least two positions. He is lethal as an out-and-out striker, but he is equally efficient playing off the main striker or in 'the hole' behind the front two.

In this role, he is more likely to be providing chances for his team-mates as well as looking for goal himself, but it means that others may be getting their name on the scoresheet through Rooney's 'assists' instead of the boy himself.

This does not seem to bother the England star. We already know he will play anywhere as long as he is playing and he genuinely enjoys the thrill of setting up a team-mate with a scintillating pass or a cross as well as hitting the back of the net himself.

In training, he often like to play in goal when the lads are winding down and has often wound up his team-mates at Manchester United by telling them that he is the club's best keeper.

ANGER MANAGEMENT

Rooney is already renowned for his volatile temper: in his short career with Everton he was sent off once and booked seventeen times. That's a disturbing figure for a boy who was still only eighteen when he left the club, so it was obvious that his new club, Manchester United, had to keep an eye on him.

His most explosive display of anger took place in Real

Madrid's Bernabeu Stadium in November 2004, when he was playing for England in a friendly against Spain.

For reasons that have never properly been explained, England's youngest player went on a one-man mission of fury against the Spanish after the hosts had taken the lead in the tenth minute.

Not for the only time, Rooney was upset with both himself and his team-mates for having conceded an early goal. And he made this clear two minutes after Spain had scored when he

Known more for outbursts against match officials, Rooney increasingly adopts a more respectful approach which does him credit.

lost possession and felled Spanish defender Joaquin. The Greek referee would have been entirely justified in booking him, but let it go.

Twenty-five minutes later, he pushed Spain's goalkeeper, Casillas, into a safety fence as the pair chased a loose ball over the line, and received a yellow card. Two minutes later, Rooney sent defender Marchena flying. All the evidence suggested that he should have been sent off for a second yellow card. But the referee, George Kasnaferis, only gave a free-kick.

The England bench realised how lucky England were to still have eleven men on the pitch and decided that Rooney, in that mood, had become a liability. They withdrew him just before half-time and brought on Alan Smith in his place.

In his last season with the club, Rooney collected more yellow cards for Everton than goals.

But the angst did not end there. The England players that night were wearing black armbands as a tribute to former national captain and Liverpool legend, Emlyn Hughes, who had passed away a few days before.

Without thinking, Rooney tore off his armband and threw it to the ground as he departed the arena. It was seen as a terrible insult to the Kop great who had won every honour in the game as well as leading his country.

He was immediately rebuked by Sven-Goran Eriksson and he quickly realised his mistake. As the players filed into the dressing room at half-time, he apologised to them and to the coaching staff.

He sat out the second-half in his England blazer behind the dugout and the following day apologised publicly for the perceived insult to Emlyn Hughes. He said he had not realised what he was doing.

His club manager, Sir Alex Ferguson, later accepted that what Rooney had done was wrong, but reminded the world that his player's explosive nature was part of the reason why he was such a fearsome player.

Rooney continued to pick up the odd booking, but came to the nation's attention again towards the end of the 2004–05 season when, while playing for United at Arsenal he went ballistic with referee Graham Poll.

Television footage clearly showed him mouthing expletives, over and over again, and Poll came in for tremendous criticism for not despatching the firebrand from the field.

I met Mr Poll the following day when he came to be interviewed at talkSPORT and he was adamant that had Rooney sworn *at him* he would definitely have sent him off. But, in fact, said Mr Poll, he may well have been seen swearing by a TV camera, but Rooney did not insult the match officials, including the ref. If he had, Poll would have sent him off.

Inevitably, Rooney did receive his marching orders in a Manchester United shirt – and it couldn't have been for a more unexpected reason.

United were playing at the Spanish club, Villarreal, in a group stage match in the Champions League. Their campaign up to that point had not been sparkling and they needed the win. They were drawing 0-0 when the referee awarded United a free-kick. Frustrated by his team's inability to score, Rooney mouthed off to the ref and was booked. As an ironic gesture, Rooney applauded the match official. And he did not do it in a subtle fashion. He clapped his black-gloved hands together right under the referee's nose. The man in black was outraged and clearly took it as a terrible personal insult to his authority, so he whipped out the yellow card again, quickly followed by the red, and Rooney was off.

It was a sorry campaign for United. They failed to pick up enough momentum in the group stage to move on to the knockout games and they were out of the top competition before Christmas.

This became a watershed for Rooney, who consciously decided that the time had come for him to get a grip of his temper. Within weeks he was seen to be adopting a different attitude to the officials.

Instead of running at them at full pelt, he started to

take a more measured approach. He would approach the referee and explain to him where he thought the ref had gone wrong; often with a physical demonstration of how he believed things had happened.

Instead of watching a young man losing control of himself with the veins in his neck bulging as if they were going to burst, we witnessed a more reflective individual who started to resemble a ballerina acting out *Swan Lake* as he tried to convince the ref that an opponent had dived or that a clash with another player had been an accident.

Rooney's renaissance was evident in both legs of United's Carling Cup semi-final against Blackburn in January.

Blackburn's *enfant-terrible* was Robbie Savage, the blond-haired, loud-mouthed, yellow-Ferrari-owning journeyman who had a reputation for winding up other players, particularly by feigning injury after the slightest contact with an opponent.

He was involved in an incident in each match which involved Rooney and which, a few months earlier, could have had serious consequences for England's talisman.

During the first match, Savage went down under a heavy tackle in a tight situation involving several players. Rooney fell on top of him. Savage made the mad decision to grab the former schoolboy boxer by the throat, at which point everybody who witnessed it thought that Rooney would retaliate immediately.

But he didn't. He pulled Savage's hands from his neck, got up and walked away. For some reason he got booked, but he even shrugged his shoulders at that.

In the return game, two weeks later, Savage was again at

the centre of an incident. There had been bad blood between himself and Rio Ferdinand throughout the first half. As the teams trooped off, Ferdinand allegedly clipped Savage about the head as he passed him to the tunnel.

Savage sprinted after him. It led to a stampede by many other players into the tunnel, but with the pull-out cover in that corner of the ground nobody could see what was going on except the ball-boys at the entrance who were apparently imitating what they were seeing by shadow-boxing with each other.

However, it later emerged that Rooney was the peacemaker who broke up the mêlée. He grabbed Savage's arm and dragged him from the main tunnel into the passage-way that leads to the dressing rooms, leaving the other players, and even the Blackburn manager, to get on with swapping insults and shouting and swearing at each other.

At the end of the game, Savage and Rooney left the field smiling and sharing a joke, although Rooney had the broader smile of the two, as United went through to the Carling Cup final.

Former top-class referee, Jeff Winter, has warned that mouthy and abusive players will be targeted at the World Cup, now and in the future. And he says that Rooney's profile is so high around the world that should he play, he is bound to be the subject of intense scrutiny by the officials.

He said, 'At the beginning of every tournament, and particularly something as important as the World Cup, the referees are gathered and given directives on what FIFA expect of them. Discipline is always high on the agenda. In the past, there has been a clampdown on red and yellow cards and a flurry of red and yellow cards has followed. With the image of the game being so important at the moment that they will be told to come down heavy on dissent, on swearing and on charging at officials.

'I can imagine the referees meeting before the first game and discussing how they will issue red cards to players running at them, mouthing off and gesticulating. The referees will be sitting there with this image of a player effing and blinding and they will think of Rooney ... His name will be very much to the fore in discussions. Remember, the common language of referees is English and they know all the unsavoury words.'

Rooney scores his team's fourth goal during the Carling Cup Final against Wigan Athletic.

NINE

CAREERING TOWARDS DESTINY...

THE PINNACLE OF The Roon's career came just thee months before the start of the World Cup in Germany and once again he proved that the bigger the stage the more he is able to demonstrate his genius.

It is a mark of the boy's greatness that he was not satisfied with his match-winning performance at the Millennium Stadium that gave him his first medal as a professional footballer.

He scored two of Manchester United's goals in their 4-0 rout of Wigan in the Carling Cup final and was unanimously given the Man of the Match award.

But he believes he should have done better. He had a header crash into the crossbar early on and also had an opportunity to grab an historic hat-trick late in the game.

Though still only twenty years of age, he is concerned that it has taken him so 'long' to get a senior medal. He last won one as a kid in the Under-13s league.

To the world at large, Wayne Rooney's adult career started on 19 October 2002. The goal he scored against Arsenal at Goodison Park that day began what has since become the Rooney legend. As commentator Clive Tyldesley screamed over the roar of the Goodison crowd, 'Remember the name – Wayne Rooney ...'

It was a shocking day for Arsenal, but a great day for Evertonians and a brilliant day for every England football fan.

Arsène Wenger had hinted that he expected his team to go through the whole season unbeaten, an ambition that, thanks to Rooney, had to be put on hold for another year. Their defeat also ended their thirty-game unbeaten run stretching way back into the previous campaign.

> **The first award Wayne received as a professional player was the October 2002 Goal of the Month award from ITV Sport. His amazing 25-yard strike against the champions Arsenal was enough to convince the judges. David Moyes presented him with the award at Bellefield.**

It wasn't just that he scored with twenty-three seconds of play remaining. It was the manner of the goal: it was an event.

Rooney, loitering in his favourite part of the pitch, just outside the penalty area, plucked the ball out of mid-air like somebody picking an apple off a tree.

No Arsenal defender saw a threat. And who could blame them? As far as they were concerned, they were being confronted by a raw young kid who had been brought on in the dying embers of the game with the score at 1-1 for a bit of first-team experience. In their eyes, he was probably a bag of nerves and posed no realistic threat to the meanest defence in the country.

The Arsenal defenders backed away to mark the men around the box. This had the effect of opening up a channel for Rooney, who now saw a clear goal-scoring opportunity.

'I knew that time was running out; I thought it was worth me having a go. I saw a gap in the top corner of the goal and just aimed for it. When the ball went in, I couldn't contain myself!'

Wayne Rooney

He steadied himself, but even as he prepared for the shot, the England keeper David Seaman didn't envisage a problem. The kid was almost 30 yards out and the goal was well covered.

A split second later, an object resembling an exocet missile flew over his head at an unbeatable speed, shaved the underneath of the cross-bar and ricocheted down over the line.

The Arsenal defenders couldn't quite believe what they had seen. Before hauling himself to his feet, Seaman sat on the ground looking sheepish and feeling foolish that he had been beaten. He wasn't to know that he had just been eclipsed by a boy who, within a few years, was going to be one of the world's great footballers and who, just four short months later, would become a fellow England international.

The goal, which became October's Goal of the Month, was scored by an apprentice footballer, five days shy of his seventeenth birthday. He had beaten Michael Owen's record as the youngest ever scorer in the Premiership by five months.

Afterwards Arsenal manager Arsène Wenger was gracious in defeat. He said, 'We have been beaten by a special goal from a special talent.'

Illustrating all the reasons why he is rightly regarded as one of the world's top club coaches he went on: 'You don't have to be a connoisseur to see that. He has everything you need for a top-class striker. I haven't seen a better striker under the age of twenty since I've been in England. He's a great prospect for English football.'

For Evertonians, it was justification of all the hope and expectancy that had been building up about Rooney over the past two to three years. They knew that he was very special. Others within the industry with their ears close to the ground were also aware of the extraordinary nature of the boy Rooney.

The previous season, he had scored eight goals in the FA Youth Cup, though even his prodigious talent could not secure the trophy for his club as the Blues were beaten in the two-legged final by Aston Villa.

It is said that, as a result of those performances alone, Manchester United, Real Madrid, Bayern Munich and AC Milan were rumoured to have been alerted by their British spies to the presence of the carrot-topped kid from Croxteth.

Everton manager David Moyes was having none of it and, as speculation and rumour developed, he made it clear that not even £15 million would be enough to interest the club in parting with their jewel.

Everton were so excited by Rooney's development

from a little schoolboy to a young man on the cusp of a brilliant senior career that they held his signing ceremony on the pitch at Goodison at half-time in their Premiership game against Derby.

He signed his scholarship contract worth £80 a week plus generous appearance and win bonuses in front of a packed Goodison Park with his mum and dad by his side.

Apart from Rooney's obvious joy, it was also *the* proudest moment for Wayne Rooney Sr and Jeanette, the heads of an Everton-daft family who, like every other parent on Merseyside, hoped that one day one of their boys would play for the club.

Again, this was all happening before Wayne had played a single game in the first team. Ironically, in light of all the other footballing records he has created, Rooney missed the opportunity to become Everton's youngest-ever debutant.

> **Wayne is an inveterate record-breaker: he's the youngest ever Everton scorer, youngest cap and youngest ever scorer for England. Rooney was also the youngest player ever to score in the European Championships in 2004 – and more than 17 million tuned in to watch, over three-quarters of the male TV audience.**

Walter Smith, Moyes' predecessor at Goodison, had wanted to play him in February of that year, but was prevented from doing so by FA rules protecting players who are still at school.

He left school the following month, but then his involvement with England in the European Under-17

Championships, where he scored five goals, stopped Moyes from picking him in May.

But these events were only postponing the inevitable: let loose in the first team in pre-season friendlies, he scored eight times in nine games, including two hat-tricks. When he finally made his debut in a competitive fixture for the first team, in Everton's opening game of the new season, a home draw with Spurs, Wayne was a fortnight older than Joe Royle had been when the club record of sixteen years and 282 days was set.

His explosion onto the football stage was not just a reward for his skill. In much the same way as Michael Jackson once said that his childhood had been 'stolen' by the fact that he was a chart-topping singer at just twelve years of age, Rooney could have claimed that his own life as a youngster had been almost totally consumed by football.

The difference is that he wanted it that way and would have had it no other. Ever since he managed to stand up on legs now worth about £25 million apiece, all he ever wanted to do was kick a football.

Wayne was not just an exceptionally rare talent. He possessed self-discipline and level-headedness that accelerated his march through the ranks in the Everton youth set-up. He looked after himself and was extremely athletic: he once, of course, considered boxing as a career and he possessed a footballing brain that many players don't develop until many years later.

When he was only fourteen, he burst into Everton's Under-19 side and scored his first goal at fifteen – the age when he received his England Under-17 call-up.

But the opportunity to stake his claim as not just a

bright prospect, but as a legend in the streets of the tiny terraced houses of his part of Liverpool came when he broke Tommy Lawton's sixty-five-year-old club record by becoming the youngest scorer when he netted two against Wrexham in the Worthington Cup at the start of October.

A month later, with the whole world now in on the secret after the Arsenal goal, Rooney travelled over the Pennines to Elland Road, where Everton had failed to beat Leeds since the day Dave Hickson made his debut in September 1951.

Rooney came on with fifteen minutes to spare and scored the only goal of the game, after beating two players. 'I am banging my head against a wall to explain

Wayne scores his second goal against Wrexham during the Worthington Cup second round match on October 1, 2002.

how Wayne Rooney scored that goal,' said Lucas Radebe, who was still picking himself off the floor when the ball hit the back of the net. 'I thought I had him. I don't know how the ball went through.'

Wayne and his strike partner Kevin Campbell were mobbed by a mini pitch invasion of demented Evertonians chanting, 'Can we play you every fifty-one years?' and 'The Queen has seen us win!'

Wayne said he felt as if he was scoring as a real footballer and, as an Evertonian, it was the best thrill in the world. That same evening he was back out in the streets kicking a ball against the wall with a gang of his mates. Panic-stricken Evertonians phoned the club to express their concerns.

Shouldn't this genius be wrapped up in cotton wool? Manager Moyes just grinned when told of the fans' anxieties. Playing with a ball was fine, he said, but if anybody saw him doing anything he shouldn't, they must send him home. It seems that the whole of the blue side of Merseyside had taken on the role of surrogate parents.

> **Wayne was the man who ended Everton's 51-year curse at Elland Road when he scored the winner against Leeds United.**

Everton travelled to St James' Park for the third round of the Worthington Cup. It was 3-3 after 120 minutes and the game went to penalties. David Unsworth's was saved, Dave Watson put his away, Rooney scored the third – despite missing two in training that morning – and Kevin Campbell finished the job. It was the first time that Everton had won a penalty shoot-out since they had beat Borussia Münchengladbach at Goodison back in 1971. (That, incidentally, proved to be disappointing in the end, as Everton went out in the next round, the quarter-finals against Panathanaikos, losing out to some questionable refereeing decisions in Greece.)

The Newcastle fans took Rooney to their heart. They compared him to their Geordie talisman, Paul Gascoigne. One Newcastle fan said at the time, 'He'll never be as daft as Gazza – but he could be as good.' With hindsight, of course, he has eclipsed Gascoigne.

There were few milestones for Rooney still to pass at club level, though he did manage to record another 'first' on Boxing Day 2002 when he was sent off in the game against Birmingham City. Many thought that it had been a very harsh decision for a relatively straightforward tackle, but what impressed everyone was that the minute the referee produced the red card, Rooney just walked without displaying a flicker of protest. He had become the youngest player to be red-carded in Premiership history.

That, however, did not prevent Sven-Goran Eriksson from including the youngster in His next full international squad.

On 12 February, he became England's youngest-ever player. He started the second half in place of Michael Owen and at seventeen years and 111 days old, he took the record that had stood for 123 years from James Prinsep of Preston, who few had previously heard of.

Sven changed almost the entire team at half-time that night and Rooney's co-striker was Everton centre-forward Frannie Jeffers, later to move on to Arsenal.

Rooney spent some of his first senior season at Everton on the bench. Davey Moyes was determined not to move him on too quickly.

But on the international scene he went from strength to strength. In April, he made his first competitive start for England and everybody was waiting for him to score his first international goal and thus become England's youngest scorer. He was awarded the Man of the Match accolade, but didn't hit the back of the net when facing Turkey at Sunderland's Stadium of Light in a Euro 2004 qualifier.

But he was a delight that night, as anybody who watched the game will confirm. He did what players so rarely do and ran at the defence. Not only was he running at them, but he was teasing them with an array of tricks that, at one stage, included what seemed to be an attempt to play 'keepy-uppy' in the middle of the pitch while powering past astonished Turkish defenders.

His performance defied logic. To have so much confidence in his first competitive game for his country was almost contrary to the normal rules of psychology. It showed, not for the first time, that one of his greatest strengths is his self-belief and his ability to settle in on any stage, no matter how big; in fact, the bigger, the better.

> **On his full debut for England against Turkey he received a standing ovation when he was substituted in the 88th minute and was later announced Man of the Match.**

Rooney had to wait until the following season – and five months – to finally snatch the youngest goalscorer record off his England colleague, Michael Owen. He did it in the away game against FYR Macedonia in another Euro 2004 game in September: he was aged seventeen years and 317 days.

> '**I didn't see Owen as a 16-year-old but I'd call him a complete striker. Rooney, on the other hand, already looks to be a complete footballer. He is strongly built with a low centre of gravity, a bit like Paul Gascoigne ... you don't have to be a connoisseur to see he's out of the ordinary.'**
>
> Arsène Wenger

Four days later, he struck for his country again in a home game against Liechtenstein and, before the end of the year, he had increased his international tally to three, by netting against Denmark in a friendly that England lost 3-2.

By contrast, he had only scored one goal for Everton by that stage of the 2003–04 season, away at Charlton. However, by the New Year, he had boosted his tally to four. By the end of the season, he was Everton's top scorer with nine goals and he scored his last goal in an Everton shirt on 13 April 2004, when he hit the net away at Leeds in the thirteenth minute to give Everton the lead.

Ironically, just after half-time, young James Milner scored the equaliser. Earlier in the season, Milner had snatched the record away from Rooney for the youngest-ever scorer in the Premiership – it is a record that he still holds.

Everton's season ended with a dispiriting away defeat at Manchester City, where they were beaten 5-1. It meant that they finished just one place above the relegation zone and one place below that day's conquerors.

Whether or not the fact that Everton had had such a dismal season had any effect on Rooney's future – one that would unfold dramatically in Portugal and throughout the summer in England – nobody can tell. But there would have been a lot of wailing and gnashing of teeth on Merseyside if anybody had realised that, as Wayne Rooney trooped off the pitch, he would never be seen in an Everton shirt again.

Less than three weeks later, he scored another two goals for his country against Iceland in a pre-Euro 2004 warm-up game. Just over a week later, Rooney lined up for the start of Euro 2004.

EURO 2004

Many doubters had expressed the view that Rooney was too young and too inexperienced to lead the England attack with Michael Owen.

Those people had no conception of Rooney's talent or his incredible will to win. To appreciate the boy's genius, you had to have been watching him for the past two years, in detail. You had to be talking to people in football and listen to those that had spent years trying to spot a talent like the Croxteth Kid.

Influential voices said that he would be overawed, that the stage would be too big, that he would shrink in the company of his peers.

Influential voices were wrong. Never in the field of football conflict has one man so dominated the course of an international competition as Wayne Rooney did in Euro 2004. With him, England were simply unstoppable. He was a goal machine, creating and scoring in equal measure.

> At Euro 2004, Wayne scored a ratio of 4 goals in 3 games in the group stage, earning Man of the Match in all three of the fixtures against France, Switzerland and Croatia.

Without him, as he was cruelly cut down in the quarter-final against Portugal, a vacuum opened up at the heart of the England team that was ruthlessly exploited by the opposition. The Portuguese knew that without him they were taking the firing pin out of a Gatling gun.

One individual who repeatedly failed to appreciate The Roon's talent was former England captain Tony Adams. He poured scorn on Rooney's two goals against Iceland and didn't think that he could fit into the England team alongside Michael Owen.

Rooney won the penalty for England in the French game and was easily England's best player, before being taken off late on. The French players were queuing up to tell their favorite journalists what a genius they had encountered in Rooney. But this was not Adams' view. He urged Sven to drop him for the next game against Switzerland. Rooney's response: he scored two goals and achieved instant world fame.

Amazingly, Adams expressed the view that Rooney should be dropped for the final group game against Croatia, reasoning that he was getting in the way of allowing Michael Owen to score. Rooney's response: he bagged another two and Michael Owen, who had not

Wayne slots home the third goal in England's 4-2 defeat of Croatia, and David Beckham shows his appreciation of the effort!

scored in the competition, spoke of how great it was to play alongside his Merseyside compatriot.

As every England fan knows, the quarter final against hosts and eventual finalists Portugal in Lisbon was there for the taking. Rooney's metatarsal injury prompted an England stagnation which, combined with some dubious refereeing, allowed Portugal to draw the game at 2-2 into extra time and at 3-3 into penalties. England lost 6-5 after Beckham and Vassell failed to convert their spotkicks.

Rooney recalled: 'It was mind-blowing. I was just in a daze afterwards – it was almost unreal, absolutely gutting. Losing on penalties is the worst feeling in the world. At the end of the night I was at the hotel, waiting for the rest of the team to come back, and was just devastated we were out of the competition.

'All the hard work, all the hopes, had ended. We genuinely believed we could go on to win the tournament if we had beaten Portugal. I am convinced we would have gone all the way, especially when you look at the teams who were knocked out – like France, Italy and Spain. So to lose like that was almost too much to take.'

Wayne, moments after his injury in Lisbon, when most fans thought he'd suffered nothing more than losing his boot in the clash with Andrade.

Rooney had gone into the last-eight clash in Lisbon as the tournament's top scorer with four goals. Euro 2004, to that date, was unquestionably the peak of Rooney's career.

But that top-of-the-world-feeling turned to the pit of despair after a clash with Jorge Andrade, who clipped the England striker's heel and left him with a broken metatarsal.

MANCHESTER UNITED

The next time Rooney put on a football shirt in competition it was that of his new club, Manchester United. And in a funny sort of a way, the broken metatarsal that he suffered in Portugal helped the transfer negotiations. He couldn't play at the start of the next season.

Everton's third game was away at United – a crucial game for them after they had suffered a dreadful 4-1 home defeat to Arsenal on the opening day.

The Arsenal result endorsed the football world's view that Everton were cannon fodder for relegation, even though they had won away at Crystal Palace in their second game.

Had Rooney been fit, then he would almost certainly have been expected to play in the bank holiday game against Manchester United which, with the transfer saga going at full revs, would have caused terrible ill will.

The deal that took the Scouser to Manchester was actually completed the next day, though it is thought that all the details had been tied up between the two clubs at the Monday lunchtime match.

Rooney's explosive introduction to his new fans is probably the greatest debut of the modern era. Bearing in mind that he had just come back from injury and that he was playing with a completely new set of team-mates, he could have been expected to ease himself in.

But that is not the way Rooney works. What happened was one of those 'were you there?' moments. It was simply stunning, as he slotted away a hat-trick against Turkish team Fenerbahce inside fifty-four minutes.

Throughout his first season, the teenager tantalised his new body of fans, his manager and his team-mates, not just with his skill but also with his incredible maturity.

His next landmark game came the following month against Arsenal.

Once again the Gunners were on a long unbeaten run. In a tense and edgy confrontation, United gained the opportunity to break the stalemate with a penalty. The second-half award was full of controversy. Rooney was said to have dived over Sol Campbell's outstretched leg, but to others it looked as though he was merely anticipating being brought down and jumped out of the way.

Van Nistelrooy put the spot-kick away and, minutes before the end, Rooney swept home a second to seal the three points.

It was a pivotal result. Arsenal, the reigning champions, were top at the time and United were only fifth, but it triggered a crisis of confidence for the Premiership holders and opened the door for Chelsea's first title in fifty years.

In November, The Roon scored two at St James' Park, the start of a remarkable record in a red shirt against Newcastle United in which he scored six goals in four league games.

The following January, the Croxteth Kid returned to Merseyside and antagonised the red half of Merseyside by scoring the only goal in United's victory. He even had a mobile phone thrown at him for his troubles.

In February, he produced an astonishing performance and steered his team to a 2-1 victory against Portsmouth with two of the best goals ever seen at Old Trafford.

The first was a scoop-come-chip over the goalkeeper from outside the area that would have done justice in its execution to a five-iron swing from Tiger Woods. His second was a volley that gave the keeper no chance.

His match-winning display lifted the club three days after they had lost at home to AC Milan in the Champions League, a result that precipitated their exit from the competition.

The previous week, he had made his first return to Goodison Park since leaving Everton. His new team beat his old one 2-0 in the fifth round of the FA Cup.

At the end of April, Rooney scored what has already been billed as one of the greatest ever Manchester United goals. (The greatest ever is generally considered to be Ryan Giggs' solo run against Arsenal in the 1999 FA Cup semi-final replay, the year United won their Treble.)

It was an astonishing 30-yard volley and was one of those six goals against the Geordies – Newcastle United. The ball came over directly from a corner.

Rooney appeared to be having a chat with the referee about a decision a few seconds earlier. Suddenly, he broke off the conversation as he saw the ball winging its way in from the left. He only took four paces before leaping into the air to smash the ball home, high in the net with his right foot. It was balletic and became the talking point of the footballing community for weeks afterwards.

The last game of his first season was a terrible

disappointment for the nineteen-year-old. Despite dominating old rivals Arsenal throughout the course of the FA Cup Final at Cardiff, United ended up losing the game on penalties. The chance to pick up his first medal in his inaugural season had gone and, afterwards, he looked dejected and lost.

Reflecting on it he said, 'I hate losing – absolutely hate it. Sir Alex has instilled in me the importance of winning. You have to win all of the time. It doesn't matter what the game is, but obviously losing a Cup Final, especially when we thought we were the better team, is very hard.'

In his second season with United, Rooney found himself visiting his boyhood spiritual home, Goodison Park, on the opening day. He scored in a 2-0 victory and, perhaps to the surprise of many, he celebrated enthusiastically in front of the Everton fans. It appeared that he was sending out two signals. To one section of the Everton fans: 'You gave me a rough time'; and to the visiting United fans: 'Just in case you had any doubts, my heart now belongs to you.'

In the long term, United's challenge for the Premiership was once again eclipsed by the unstoppable force that Chelsea had become. And, by Christmas, the European campaign was over. Portugal was proving The Roon's unlucky country, as Benfica of Lisbon finished United off just as they were to dispose of Liverpool in the following round.

However, Rooney's single-minded approach to his football was never better illustrated than when he lined up against Arsenal at the end of last season.

United were still in with a shout of the title. Champions Chelsea were perceived at the time to be on the verge of a 'wobble' and were just seven points ahead of United at the top of the Premiership.

On the day Chelsea were playing West Ham at home. On paper that was a fairly comfortable fixture and they were expected to win the Sunday afternoon two o'clock kick-off.

United had the much tougher fixture, entertaining an in-form Arsenal at Old Trafford later in the day. It was vital that they took the three points, irrespective of Chelsea's result.

But the focal point of the day's events drifted away from the pure art of football as soon as the Sunday newspapers dropped onto millions of door-mats all over the country.

Rooney was alleged to have racked up gambling debts of £700,000, a figure later accepted by his personal management team. He had wagered huge sums on all forms of sporting results, except for matches in which he and his team were involved.

And it transpired that the money was owed to a man who was a close business associate of Michael Owen. Rooney's England striking partner had supposedly introduced his business manager Stephen Smith to his Merseyside pal who could deal with footballers betting activities out of the public eye.

As soon as the story broke there was speculation that the close bond between England's two top strikers had been fractured.

Providing both are fit they are likely to be England's first choice strike-force for many years to come. In particular, much of the Germany 06 campaign had been built on their potency and goal-getting ability.

How then was this emerging saga going to affect Rooney as it unfolded hours before one of United's most important games of the season?

The pressure increased after Chelsea blew West Ham away 4-1. Not only did they comprehensively beat the east Londoners but they also overcame an early goal against them and a sending off that reduced them to ten men in the first half.

As the Chelsea game finished the United duel kicked off 200 miles to the north. It was vital that the reds took all three points to keep up any hope of pipping Chelsea for the Premiership crown.

Any doubts about whether or not Rooney was distracted disappeared very early on. He was at his best, peppering the Arsenal goal with shots from every angle, drawing the very best out of keeper Jens Lehmann.

In the 43rd minute an incident occurred which twelve months earlier could have sent Rooney into a lather.

Ruud van Nistlerooy stroked a delightful ball into his strike partner's path on the edge of the area and to the left of the goal. Rooney hit it goalwards but it shaved the post.

At first it looked as though he had simply misjudged the angle but immediately he started protesting to the referee, indicating that somebody had handled the ball.

The problem was that his shot was so fierce and the ball travelled so rapidly that the human eye could not pick out what had happened. Several TV replays later from six different angles revealed that Arsenal defender Kolo Toure had dived across the flight of the ball and tipped it with his hands on to the post.

This was a dreadful infringement. United and Rooney had been denied a goal and possibly the advantage of having the Arsenal man sent off for handling in the area.

As the score was still 0-0 at the time and it was a few minute from the break, which is the best psychological time for a team to score – and the worst to concede – it was a crucial moment.

Thinking back to the England game in Northern Ireland when Rooney exploded in frustration at being played out of position, it might not have been unexpected if he had blown up at this significant injustice.

And with that morning's newspaper headlines still fresh in everybody's mind, was the tinder-box about to ignite?

It didn't. In fact, after his initial and quite legitimate protest to referee Graham Poll, he accepted that nobody had seen it except himself.

It showed a new level of maturity in the boy. Nobody could really blame the officials. Even in a dozen TV replays you had to look really hard to spot the hand-ball. But if Arsenal thought they had got away with it they were wrong. Early in the second-half Mikael Silvestre floated over a made-to-measure cross which dipped over the head of Arsenal defender Senderos.

Rooney brought it down with an exquisite touch and before any other defender had a chance to react he lashed the ball into the net with a force that resembled a shell coming out of the barrel of a warship's big gun.

It was simply unstoppable.

Twenty minutes later Rooney took Arsenal's full-back down the right wing and squared the ball for team-mate Ji Sung Park to fire home.

According to statisticians, Wayne Rooney travels around 11.82km during a match, more than the average even for a midfielder. He walks for 4000m, jogs for 4800m, runs for 1500m, and sprints for the same distance. It has been calculated that, on average, Wayne heads the ball twice, uses his chest 13 times and his feet touch the ball 90 times in one game.

Relaxed enough in the preceding training session, Wayne lost his temper in the game against Spain.

Rooney was voted Man of the Match and the odds on him being voted the PFA Player of the Year two weeks later shortened to make him favourite.

Asked after the game if the gambling debt headlines had been playing on his mind, he answered: 'I think my performance out their today answers that question.

'We knew Chelsea had won before we kicked off so that put extra pressure on us to get the result today. All we can do is to keep on winning.'

Later that day Rooney let it be known that the gambling issue would have no effect on his friendship and his playing partnership with Michael Owen.

Rooney tries to dig his team out of a Denmark-shaped hole, to no avail.

Later in the season, Manchester United's fierce rivals on Merseyside halted their FA Cup ambitions when they beat United 1-0 in the fifth round of the FA Cup at Anfield. That meant it was all down to the League Cup final against Wigan for that elusive medal.

As a club, Wigan had never been on such an elevated platform. In the event, United crushed them 4-0. Rooney got the first and the last.

He was easily the Man of the Match and, for the first time, he felt the elation of being a trophy winner.

ENGLAND

On the international front, Rooney did not resume his England career until October 2004 against Wales.

The following month, he was involved in his most controversial game to date for his country. In an away friendly in Spain, he had to be substituted before half time for fear that he was about to get himself sent off.

The next time he scored for his country, the team also lost in a friendly. In a débâcle of a performance, England were beaten 4-1 in Denmark.

The squad then resumed their World Cup qualifying games. They secured their place in Germany against Austria with a game to spare and then, vitally, won their group by beating Poland in the last game.

The last part of the campaign was not without incident, though. In Northern Ireland, England suffered one of the worst defeats in their history, going down 1-0.

That game will be best remembered for the England players falling out with each other and Rooney, in particular, for becoming frustrated with what appeared to be a shifting gameplan.

At one point, he clearly expressed his views to a number of his team-mates and was even said to have had an angry clash with captain David Beckham. Whatever problems arose, they didn't last long as, a few weeks later, Rooney and Coleen were pictured in Beckham's private box inside Real Madrid's Bernabeu Stadium.

'It was a tough game in Northern Ireland and I was disappointed with the way that I handled myself. But if the time comes when I am not disappointed when things are not going right – that's when people should worry,' he told the *Mirror*.

Rooney has had to make a seismic change in his life by the age of twenty. Born and brought up an Evertonian, he was instantly converted to a 'Manc' the moment he signed for the Reds.

That was not disloyalty to his boyhood club. It was just his ruthless ambition that some people find difficult to accept, because it is completely out of sync with his youth.

But Rooney is different. His life has changed and he is completely immersed in his new existence.

So when he says, 'One of the outstanding memories of my season is going back to beat my old team, Everton,' he is just being brutally honest. He has moved on and sentiment has no part in his present.

That's not to say that he hasn't lost some of his schoolboy instincts. Asked how he felt about Liverpool winning their fifth European Cup he replied, 'It was horrible and I was very jealous. I was desperate for Liverpool to be beaten and, when they were 3-0 down at half-time, I had a huge smile on my face – but they came back.'

David Beckham tries to calm Wayne as Northern Ireland stun England.

In the run-up to Germany 2006, he dismissed all thoughts except those of ultimate victory. He had conviction that the squad in which he plays is of World Cup-winning quality. He has no fear if, should he play, the opposition want to pay him special attention.

'I don't mind if teams want to man-mark me or stick two men on me. I can handle that. No problem. It gives Michael Owen more space and hopefully he can use it to score goals, which he's very capable of doing.'

He summed himself up in a few choice and revealing words. 'When I am on the pitch, I am not scared of anything. I just play my own game ...'

And Wayne Rooney's game remains quite simple – to be the best football player in the world.

ROONEY PLAYING STATISTICS

2002-03 SEASON

Date	Competition	Home	Score	Away	Rooney Goals	Cards
17/08/02	Premiership	Everton	2-2	Tottenham	0	
24/08/02	Premiership	Sunderland	0-1	Everton	0	
28/08/02	Premiership	Everton	1-1	Birmingham	0	
31/08/02	Premiership	Man City	3-1	Everton	0	
11/09/02	Premiership	Southampton	1-0	Everton	0	
14/09/02	Premiership	Everton	2-1	Middlesbrough	0	
22/09/02	Premiership	Aston Villa	3-2	Everton	0	
01/10/02	League Cup	Wrexham	0-3	Everton	2	
07/10/02	Premiership	Manchester United	3-0	Everton	0	
19/10/02	Premiership	Everton	2-1	Arsenal	1	Yellow
27/10/02	Premiership	West Ham	0-1	Everton	0	Yellow
03/11/02	Premiership	Leeds	0-1	Everton	1	
06/11/02	League Cup	Newcastle	3-3	Everton	0	Yellow
09/11/02	Premiership	Everton	1-0	Charlton	0	Yellow
17/11/02	Premiership	Blackburn	0-1	Everton	0	
23/11/02	Premiership	Everton	1-0	West Bromwich Albion	0	
01/12/02	Premiership	Newcastle	2-1	Everton	0	
04/12/02	League Cup	Chelsea	4-1	Everton	0	
07/12/02	Premiership	Everton	1-3	Chelsea	0	

Date	Competition	Home	Score	Away	Rooney Goals	Cards
14/12/02	Premiership	Everton	2-1	Blackburn	1	
22/12/02	Premiership	Liverpool	0-0	Everton	0	
26/12/02	Premiership	Birmingham	1-1	Everton	0	Red
28/12/02	Premiership	Everton	0-0	Bolton	0	
01/01/03	Premiership	Everton	2-2	Man City	0	
04/01/03	FA Cup	Shrewsbury	2-1	Everton	0	Yellow
08/02/03	Premiership	Charlton	2-1	Everton	0	Yellow
12/02/03	International	England	1-3	Australia	0	
22/02/03	Premiership	Everton	2-1	Southampton	0	
01/03/03	Premiership	Middlesbrough	1-1	Everton	0	
15/03/03	Premiership	Everton	0-0	West Ham	0	
23/03/03	Premiership	Arsenal	2-1	Everton	1	
29/03/03	European Championships	Liechtenstein	0-2	England	0	
02/04/03	European Championships	England	2-0	Turkey	0	
06/04/03	Premiership	Everton	2-1	Newcastle	1	
12/04/03	Premiership	West Bromwich Albion	1-2	Everton	0	Yellow
19/04/03	Premiership	Everton	1-2	Liverpool	0	
21/04/03	Premiership	Chelsea	4-1	Everton	0	
26/04/03	Premiership	Everton	2-1	Aston Villa	1	

Date	Competition	Home	Score	Away	Rooney Goals	Cards
03/05/03	Premiership	Fulham	2-0	Everton	0	
11/05/03	Premiership	Everton	1-2	Manchester United	0	Yellow
03/06/03	International	England	2-1	Serbia Montenegro	0	
11/06/03	European Championships	England	2-1	Slovakia	0	
TOTALS:	**GOALS: 8**		**YELLOW CARDS: 8**	**RED CARDS: 1**		

2003-04 SEASON

Date	Competition	Home	Score	Away	Rooney Goals	Cards
16/08/03	Premiership	Arsenal	2-1	Everton	0	Yellow
23/08/03	Premiership	Everton	3-1	Fulham	0	
26/08/03	Premiership	Charlton	2-2	Everton	1	Yellow
30/08/03	Premiership	Everton	0-3	Liverpool	0	Yellow
06/09/03	European Championships	Macedonia	1-2	England	1	
10/09/03	European Championships	England	2-0	Liechtenstein	1	
13/09/03	Premiership	Everton	2/2	Newcastle	0	
21/09/03	Premiership	Middlesbrough	1-0	Everton	0	Yellow
24/09/03	League Cup	Everton	3-0	Stockport	0	

ROONEY TUNES

Date	Competition	Home	Score	Away	Rooney Goals	Cards
28/09/03	Premiership	Everton	4-0	Leeds	0	
04/10/03	Premiership	Tottenham	3-0	Everton	0	Yellow
11/10/03	European Championships	Turkey	0-0	England	0	
25/10/03	Premiership	Aston Villa	0-0	Everton	0	
29/10/03	League Cup	Everton	1-0	Charlton	0	
01/11/03	Premiership	Everton	0-1	Chelsea	0	
16/11/03	International	England	2-3	Denmark	1	
22/11/03	Premiership	Everton	2-0	Wolves	0	
29/11/03	Premiership	Bolton	2-0	Everton	0	
03/12/03	League Cup	Middlesbrough	0-0	Everton	0	
07/12/03	Premiership	Everton	0-0	Man City	0	
13/12/03	Premiership	Portsmouth	1-2	Everton	1	Yellow
20/12/03	Premiership	Everton	3-2	Leicester	1	
26/12/03	Premiership	Manchester United	3-2	Everton	0	Yellow
28/12/03	Premiership	Everton	1-0	Birmingham	1	
03/01/04	FA Cup	Everton	3-1	Norwich	0	
07/01/04	Premiership	Everton	1-1	Arsenal	0	
10/01/04	Premiership	Fulham	2-1	Everton	0	
17/01/04	Premiership	Everton	0-1	Charlton	0	

254

ROONEY PLAYING STATISTICS

Date	Competition	Home	Score	Away	Rooney Goals	Cards
25/01/04	FA Cup	Everton	1-1	Fulham	0	Yellow
31/01/04	Premiership	Liverpool	0-0	Everton	0	
04/02/04	FA Cup	Fulham	2-1	Everton	0	
07/02/04	Premiership	Everton	3-4	Manchester United	0	
11/02/04	Premiership	Birmingham	3-0	Everton	0	
18/02/04	International	Portugal	1-1	England	0	
21/02/04	Premiership	Southampton	3-3	Everton	2	
28/02/04	Premiership	Everton	2-0	Aston Villa	0	Yellow
13/03/04	Premiership	Everton	1-0	Portsmouth	1	
20/03/04	Premiership	Leicester	1-1	Everton	1	Yellow
27/03/04	Premiership	Everton	1-1	Middlesbrough	0	
31/03/04	International	Sweden	1-0	England	0	
13/04/04	Premiership	Leeds	1-1	Everton	1	
17/04/04	Premiership	Chelsea	0-0	Everton	0	
24/04/04	Premiership	Everton	0-1	Blackburn	0	
01/05/04	Premiership	Wolves	2-1	Everton	0	Yellow
08/05/04	Premiership	Everton	1-2	Bolton	0	
15/05/04	Premiership	Man City	5-1	Everton	0	Yellow
01/06/04	International	England	1-1	Japan	0	
05/06/04	International	England	6-1	Iceland	2	

Date	Competition	Home	Score	Away	Rooney Goals	Cards
13/06/04	European Championships	France	2-1	England	0	
17/06/04	European Championships	England	3-0	Switzerland	2	Yellow
21/06/04	European Championships	Croatia	2-4	England	2	
24/06/04	European Championships	Portugal	2-2	England	0	
TOTALS:	GOALS: 18	YELLOW CARDS: 13	RED CARDS: 0			

2004-05 SEASON

Date	Competition	Home	Score	Away	Rooney Goals	Cards
28/09/04	European Cup	Manchester United	6-2	Fenerbahce	3	
03/10/04	Premiership	Manchester United	1-1	Middlesbrough	0	
09/10/04	World Cup	England	2-0	Wales	0	
13/10/04	World Cup	Azerbaijan	0-1	England	0	Yellow
16/10/04	Premiership	Birmingham	0-0	Manchester United	0	
19/10/04	European Cup	Sparta Prague	0-0	Manchester United	0	
24/10/04	Premiership	Manchester United	2-0	Arsenal	1	
30/10/04	Premiership	Portsmouth	2-0	Manchester United	0	Yellow

256

ROONEY PLAYING STATISTICS

Date	Competition	Home	Score	Away	Rooney Goals	Cards
03/11/04	European Cup	Manchester United	4-1	Sparta Prague	0	
07/11/04	Premiership	Manchester United	0-0	Man City	0	
14/11/04	Premiership	Newcastle	1-3	Manchester United	2	
17/11/04	International	Spain	1-0	England	0	Yellow
20/11/04	Premiership	Manchester United	2-0	Charlton	0	
23/11/04	European Cup	Manchester United	2-1	Lyon	0	
27/11/04	Premiership	West Bromwich Albion	0-3	Manchester United	0	
04/12/04	Premiership	Manchester United	3-0	Southampton	1	
13/12/04	Premiership	Fulham	1-1	Manchester United	0	
18/12/04	Premiership	Manchester United	5-2	C Palace	0	
26/12/04	Premiership	Manchester United	2-0	Bolton	0	
28/12/04	Premiership	Aston Villa	0-1	Manchester United	0	
12/01/05	League Cup	Chelsea	0-0	Manchester United	0	
15/01/05	Premiership	Liverpool	0-1	Manchester United	1	Yellow
19/01/05	FA Cup	Exeter	0-2	Manchester United	1	
22/01/05	Premiership	Manchester United	3-1	Aston Villa	0	
26/01/05	League Cup	Manchester United	1-2	Chelsea	0	
29/01/05	FA Cup	Manchester United	3-0	Middlesbrough	2	
01/02/05	Premiership	Arsenal	2-4	Manchester United	0	Yellow
05/02/05	Premiership	Manchester United	2-0	Birmingham	1	

257

Date	Competition	Home	Score	Away	Rooney Goals	Cards
09/02/05	International	England	0-0	Holland	0	
13/02/05	Premiership	Man City	0-2	Manchester United	1	Yellow
19/02/05	FA Cup	Everton	0-2	Manchester United	0	
23/02/05	European Cup	Manchester United	0-1	Milan	0	
26/02/05	Premiership	Manchester United	2-1	Portsmouth	2	
05/03/05	Premiership	C Palace	0-0	Manchester United	0	
08/03/05	European Cup	Milan	1-0	Manchester United	0	
12/03/05	FA Cup	Southampton	0-4	Manchester United	0	
19/03/05	Premiership	Manchester United	1-0	Fulham	0	
26/03/05	World Cup	England	4-0	Northern Ireland	0	
30/03/05	World Cup	England	2-0	Azerbaijan	0	
02/04/05	Premiership	Manchester United	0-0	Blackburn	0	
09/04/05	Premiership	Norwich	2-0	Manchester United	0	Yellow
17/04/05	FA Cup	Newcastle	1-4	Manchester United	0	
20/04/05	Premiership	Everton	1-0	Manchester United	0	
24/04/05	Premiership	Manchester United	2-1	Newcastle	1	Yellow
01/05/05	Premiership	Charlton	0-4	Manchester United	1	
07/05/05	Premiership	Manchester United	1-1	West Bromwich Albion	0	
10/05/05	Premiership	Manchester United	1-3	Chelsea	0	
15/05/05	Premiership	Southampton	1-2	Manchester United	0	

ROONEY PLAYING STATISTICS

Date	Competition	Home	Score	Away	Rooney Goals	Cards
21/05/05	FA Cup	Arsenal	0-0	Manchester United	0	
TOTALS:	**GOALS: 17**		**YELLOW CARDS: 8**	**RED CARDS: 0**		

2004-05 SEASON

Date	Competition	Home	Score	Away	Rooney Goals	Cards
09/08/05	European Cup	Manchester United	3-0	Debreceni VSC	1	
13/08/05	Premiership	Everton	0-2	Manchester United	1	
17/08/05	International	Denmark	4-1	England	1	
20/08/05	Premiership	Manchester United	1-0	Aston Villa	0	Yellow
28/08/05	Premiership	Newcastle	0-2	Manchester United	1	
03/09/05	World Cup	Wales	0-1	England	0	
07/09/05	World Cup	Northern Ireland	1-0	England	0	Yellow
10/09/05	Premiership	Manchester United	1-1	Man City	0	
14/09/05	European Cup	Villarreal	0-0	Manchester United	0	Red
18/09/05	Premiership	Liverpool	0-0	Manchester United	0	
24/09/05	Premiership	Manchester United	1-2	Blackburn	0	
01/10/05	Premiership	Fulham	2-3	Manchester United	1	
12/10/05	World Cup	England	2-1	Poland	0	

259

Date	Competition	Home	Score	Away	Rooney Goals	Cards
15/10/05	Premiership	Sunderland	1-3	Manchester United	1	
22/10/05	Premiership	Manchester United	1-1	Tottenham	0	Yellow
29/10/05	Premiership	Middlesbrough	4-1	Manchester United	0	
02/11/05	European Cup	Lille	1-0	Manchester United	0	Yellow
06/11/05	Premiership	Manchester United	1-0	Chelsea	0	
12/11/05	International	Argentina	2-3	England	1	
19/11/05	Premiership	Charlton	1-3	Manchester United	0	
22/11/05	European Cup	Manchester United	0-0	Villarreal	0	
27/11/05	Premiership	West Ham	1-2	Manchester United	1	Yellow
03/12/05	Premiership	Manchester United	3-0	Portsmouth	1	
07/12/05	European Cup	Benfica	2-1	Manchester United	0	
11/12/05	Premiership	Manchester United	1-1	Everton	0	
14/12/05	Premiership	Manchester United	4-0	Wigan	2	
17/12/05	Premiership	Aston Villa	0-2	Manchester United	1	
20/12/05	League Cup	Birmingham	1-3	Manchester United	0	
26/12/05	Premiership	Manchester United	3-0	West Bromwich Albion	0	
28/12/05	Premiership	Birmingham	2-2	Manchester United	1	
31/12/05	Premiership	Manchester United	4-1	Bolton	0	
03/01/06	Premiership	Arsenal	0-0	Manchester United	0	Yellow
08/01/06	FA Cup	Burton Albion	0-0	Manchester United	0	
11/01/06	League Cup	Blackburn	1-1	Manchester United	0	Yellow

ROONEY PLAYING STATISTICS

Date	Competition	Home	Score	Away	Rooney Goals	Cards
14/01/06	Premiership	Man City	3-1	Manchester United	0	Yellow
22/01/06	Premiership	Manchester United	1-0	Liverpool	0	Yellow
25/01/06	League Cup	Manchester United	2-1	Blackburn	0	
29/01/06	FA Cup	Wolves	0-3	Manchester United	0	
01/02/06	Premiership	Blackburn	4-3	Manchester United	0	
04/02/06	Premiership	Manchester United	4-2	Fulham	0	
11/02/06	Premiership	Portsmouth	1-3	Manchester United	0	
18/02/06	FA Cup	Liverpool	1-0	Manchester United	0	
26/02/06	League Cup	Manchester United	4-0	Wigan	2	
01/03/06	International	England	2-1	Uruguay	0	
06/03/06	Premiership	Wigan	1-2	Manchester United	2	
12/03/06	Premiership	Manchester United	2-0	Newcastle	0	
18/03/06	Premiership	West Bromwich Albion	1-2	Manchester United	1	
26/03/06	Premiership	Manchester United	3-0	Birmingham	0	
29/03/06	Premiership	Manchester United	1-0	West Ham	0	
01/04/06	Premiership	Bolton	1-2	Manchester United	0	Yellow
09/04/06	Premiership	Manchester United	2-0	Arsenal	1	
14/04/06	Premiership	Manchester United	0-0	Sunderland	0	
17/04/06	Premiership	Tottenham	1-2	Manchester United	2	
29/04/06	Premiership	Chelsea	3-0	Manchester United	0	Yellow
TOTALS:	**GOALS: 21**	**YELLOW CARDS: 11**	**RED CARDS: 1**			

ACKNOWLEDGEMENTS

My thanks to Sue Evison, without whose inspirational and ground-breaking work with Wayne Rooney and Coleen McLoughlin, I could never have put a book together. Thanks to Paul Wood, the top illustrator. And to Giles Carruthers for his dogged research. I'm also grateful to everybody who shared with me their admiration of Wayne Rooney – the world's greatest footballer.